The Case for Creativity

CANNES LIONS, LONDON

WWW.CANNESLIONS.COM

First published 2011 by AUT Media
Second edition, 2016

© 2016 Cannes Lions
ISBN: 978-0-9935082-0-2

The Case for Creativity

JAMES HURMAN

Praise for *The Case for Creativity*

"An inspiring round-up of the best thinking from the last three decades. James Hurman excels at joining up the dots between eras and geographies. His message is the more powerful for being so well researched. Practitioner-led, powered by data, his case for creativity is utterly convincing. Business will be the richer for embracing this thinking."

— *Janet Hull OBE, IPA Director of Marketing Strategy & Chairman IPA Databank*

"A must read for anyone who needs to understand the indivisible link between creativity and commerce."

— *Gareth Kay, Co-Founder, Chapter San Francisco*

"After reading The Case for Creativity, I came away with better evidence than before on a theory that I've long believed in. I recommend it to everyone in our industry and beyond."

— *Paul Donaldson, Strategy Director, Carlton & United Breweries/SAB Miller, Australia*

"A great read… a timely and important contribution to the marketing debate… it should become mandatory reading for all clients."

— *Michael Burgess, General Manager, Marketing, Weight Watchers Australasia*

"The book I wish I'd written."

— *Donald Gunn, founder, The Gunn Report*

"Bloody good… Hurman has brought together compelling arguments demonstrating the success of businesses that have shown creative courage."

— *Idealog Magazine*

"This is an important book written by someone who is as far as you can get from being an advertising luvvie about how communications work."

— *Directory Magazine*

"A remarkably easy read and a good introduction to how advertising should work."

— *Unlimited Magazine*

Contents

Foreword

Keith Weed, Chief Marketing &
Communications Officer, Unilever

Leading brands and agencies have known for many years that more creative work delivers better results than 'safe' and rational advertising. What has been exciting in more recent times is to see the emerging proof of this; the hard evidence that creative work is more memorable, more effective and more able to drive overall business performance.

What James Hurman has done with this book is to bring all this evidence together in such a compelling way that no one can be in any doubt. Read this and there is no need for any further debate; it is simply evident that more creative communications undeniably drive more successful outcomes.

I have no doubt that creativity drives effectiveness. And in this increasingly cluttered world, that creativity is becoming even more important not only to engage people, but even to be seen. It is a core requirement for every marketing communication.

In fact, looking back now it seems incredible that there was ever any doubt. It only takes a moment to recall the greatest advertising campaigns and realise how many of them used creativity to tell emotional stories that captured the imagination or – as in our case at Unilever – increasingly used creativity to tell a powerful story with an empowering sense of purpose.

At Unilever, our focus has moved on to using creativity throughout our business to enable us to help build a brighter future. I believe that marketers and advertising agencies need to step up to this challenge. We can no longer have marketers in one corner trying to sell more stuff and a sustainability department in another corner trying to save the planet. We need to creatively develop new, transformational business models that enable us to build a better future through sustainable brands with a strong purpose.

And I look forward to the day when we have a book that collects the proof that these new sustainable business models are working in the way that, finally, and beyond all reasonable doubt, this important book definitively demonstrates creativity drives business performance.

Introduction to the 2016 edition

I remember Brent Smart, then Managing Director of Colenso BBDO, coming home from the Cannes Lions in 2008 really fired up. It happens to everyone in Cannes. You go, you see wall-to-wall amazing work, and you leave making lists of the things you'll do when you get home to make your own work better. When Smarty came home to New Zealand, he planned a meeting with one of the agency's biggest but least creative clients. He pulled all that great work he'd seen together, and invited the client's entire marketing team into the agency one afternoon to drink beer and look at the work, sure that it would inspire them as it had him.

We sat together in our boardroom and looked at Alex Bogusky's 'Whopper Freakout', Dave Droga's 'Million' campaign and Saatchi's great 'You can say anything with a smile' Crest ads.

We watched, we talked, we laughed, we oohed and aahed. Then Smarty popped the question. "So, who wants to make work that'll win a Cannes Lion next year?"

There must have been about 15 of them, clustered around their marketing director, a Rhodes Scholar with a stiff imagination. The session had gone well – they'd obviously enjoyed themselves – and I was expecting their hands to shoot up. But they looked nervous. One person half-raised their hand, then looked at the marketing director and lowered it again.

It was a horrible moment. Smarty genuinely believed the client would be more successful if the work was better, and had faithfully collected up the best work he could find to share with them in an attempt at bonding, aligning and, together, improving. They'd nodded along, but when it came down to it, left him hanging. For all its novelty, creativity just wasn't something that they viewed as important to their success.

We both left the meeting feeling completely deflated, and the moment really stuck with me as a sign of the times. In 2008 we were an industry divided between those who believed in creativity and those who were sceptical of it. It struck me as a deeply unhealthy contradiction. As somebody who loves creativity, I felt defensive of great work; but as a planner I could also understand the client community's need to see some evidence before throwing themselves behind a more creative approach. The fact that nobody had popularised that evidence struck me as a golden opportunity.

Just four years later so much had changed. Peter Field had published his seminal work proving that creatively awarded work was 11 times as efficient as non-awarded work. Jim Stengel at P&G and Jonathan Mildenhall at Coca-Cola had led creative revolutions inside their revered organisations. Word had spread and the culture throughout the industry had reached a tipping point.

After this book was first published, I was privileged to speak with senior people from many of the world's largest marketing organisations – and all of them told me that becoming more creative was central to their strategy. Most of them struggled with how to actually do it, with many still shying away from buying truly great work. But the belief and the intention were there – and I got so much joy from the feeling that the back of the problem may have been broken.

Another four years on, I've had the chance to revisit what I found when I wrote the first edition. I can't say it wasn't a little daunting. What if creativity proved to be less effective now?

For this edition I needed to look at new Gunn Report and effectiveness-award data to see if the most creative agencies were still the most effective. I needed to see what Peter Field had found out in his continued mining of the IPA's databank. And I needed to look at the Cannes Lions Creative Marketer of the Year companies and see if they were still outperforming the stock market.

If any of those new analyses didn't work out, well, I'd be in trouble. But, as you've probably already guessed, they all did. The most creative agencies remain well ahead of less creative agencies in terms of their ability to product effective work. The Creative Marketer of the Year companies continue to decisively beat the S&P 500 and teach us so much about how to activate creativity and innovation within large organisations.

And in addition to Peter's early findings remaining consistent with today's data, he has uncovered new insight into how highly creative campaigns can be even more effective.

The other point that stands is that creativity supercharges great strategy, as opposed to being a replacement for it. The idea that 'all you need to do to be effective is win a creative award' is not the intention of this book. All the best campaigns are great strategic ideas before they're great creative executions.

And of course, creativity will always be something that some do better than others. Conceiving, selling and producing Lion-winning work is extremely difficult at the best of times. As is buying it – and despite wanting great work, some clients' eyes will always be too big for their organisations' stomachs.

But it not being wanted in the first place was an enormous hurdle. It was once fashionable for marketers to erect that hurdle, but we've all grown up a little, and it makes me happy that it's been a long time since I've found myself in a meeting like that one back in 2008.

I hope this book will continue to be a mouthpiece for the excellent job that people throughout our industry have done proving the value of creativity. I hope you enjoy the read, and that it helps you in your own journey toward better, more effective work.

Couzens & Ingram's *Wicked Sick BMX*

The case for this book

"Nobody reads advertising. People read what interests them,
and sometimes it's an ad."

— *Howard Luck Gossage, Gossage, Freeman & Partners, San Francisco*

In 2009 a pair of advertising creatives from Australia set out to resolve one of their industry's oldest uncertainties: Does creativity make advertising more effective?

Ben Couzens and Jim Ingram chose an ordinary product – a BMX bike that was for sale on eBay. It had an ordinary ad: 'Up for sale is a reliance boomerang BMX. Quite rare. Some rust on forks and bars. Pick up only from Clayton. Happy Bidding.'

They bought that ordinary BMX for the ordinary price of $27.50. Then they conducted an experiment in which they sold the exact same product in the exact same medium, but this time added creativity.

Their ad went like this:[1]

BMX Super Rad Extreme 2000
This is a max wicked sick BMX.
It's a Reliance Boomerang and it's done heaps of maximum extreme stunts. I have mostly done stunts on this bike since forever. Once I did a boom gnarly stunt trick and a girl got pregnant just by watching my extremeness to the maxxxx.
Some details about sickmax BMX:
Comes with everything you see including:
TOPS AS SUSPENSION REAR FORKS!! 2 x wheels. 1 x seat. I will even throw in my sick BMXing name for FREE – Wicked Styx.
Has minor surface rust on handlebars and front forks (easily removed). More rust on rear forks (as shown in pics). Tyres hold air but are pretty old.
Basically, it's an old BMX, but its radness is still 100% in tact.
Tricks I have done on this BMX:
Endos – 234
Sick Wheelies – 687
Skids – 143,000
Bunny Hops – 2 (My brother dared me to do them, which I did because I'm Rad to the power of Sick.)
Flipouts – 28
Basically if you buy this bike you will become a member to every club that was ever invented, worldwide, because you will be awesome.

On day one the bids reached $55, double what had been paid for the bike. Dozens of enquiries came in. "How long are the skids that this bike can do?" asked one bidder. "The skids odometer shows 128,992 metres," Ben replied, "but once I did a skid that went for two weeks."

On day two there were numerous blog posts with titles like 'one of the best eBay ads I've ever seen'.

By day three the ad's copy had made its way into the Australian vernacular. "This apple fritter is rad to the power of sick!" tweeted a Twitterer midway through his snack. "JP O'Brien once did a BMX skid that went for two weeks," boasted JP O'Brien on Facebook.

The bike finally sold for $134.50 – nearly five times the previous sale value of the product – demonstrating the value of creativity, at least in selling BMX bikes on eBay.

Much has been said about the need for creativity in advertising. Perhaps the most lucid advice is Bill Bernbach's timeless observation: "if your advertising goes unnoticed, everything else is academic."

And let's be honest, quite a lot of advertising goes unnoticed. Consider your last 24 hours. You will have been exposed to countless ads. In 2007, Yankelovich Research estimated that city dwellers were exposed to over 3,000 commercial messages each day.[2] How many can you recall right now? One per cent? That's 30. Go on, have a try.

Harvard University research shows that, of the thousands of ads that marketers pay for us to be exposed to each day, we're oblivious to all but 76. And it isn't that we actively choose not to engage with the rest –

rather our subconscious filters them out so effectively that we're completely unaware of them. Then, of the 76 ads that make it through, just 12 make any sort of impression on us. And finally, of those 12, it's unusual for us to be able to recall more than two of them the next day.[3]

American businessman John Wanamaker famously said, "I know that half of my advertising dollars are wasted... I just don't know which half." If Harvard and Yankelovich are right, we're wasting somewhat more than half our advertising dollars.

So why does so much advertising go unnoticed?

"Nobody reads advertising," said Howard Luck Gossage, the great San Francisco adman. "People read what interests them, and sometimes it's an ad."

The classic case for creativity is that it's something of a Trojan horse. It takes a marketing message and wraps it up in an idea interesting enough to avoid going unnoticed. Interesting enough to stand out among a barrage of commercial messages too dense for any normal person to even begin to negotiate.

"This is a really nice idea," a senior client said to me once. "I like it a lot. But it's getting in the way of the product message. We just need to clearly communicate that message."

It's easy to succumb to the belief that when consumers are distracted from what they're doing by an ad, they're in a state of 'paying attention'. That as long as we communicate a message clearly to them, they'll listen, learn, and buy.

Even the most conventional wisdom suggests this isn't the case. Yet as logical as the arguments for creativity are, scepticism is rife.

In 1995, academics published in the Journal of Advertising Research noted that "within the advertising industry, there seems to be a never-ending struggle between those who create the advertising ('creatives') and those advertising managers who insist that it be 'effective'."[4]

Their observation reflects a belief from some corners of our industry that creativity and effectiveness are two separate and unrelated outcomes. It's a belief held emphatically by some. In 2006 the marketing head of a major German FMCG company told McKinsey & Company that "creativity is irrelevant at best. Often, it is downright harmful to advertising success."[5]

The sceptical opinion is that creativity is a sort of irresponsible folly that creatives attempt to get past unwitting clients in order to win awards. That creativity has little if anything to do with making advertising more effective. That agencies who pursue highly creative ideas are quite knowingly sabotaging their clients' chances of success.

It's true that creative people are highly motivated by their own passion for creativity and the creative awards system that recognises their level of achievement among their peers. But is that really evidence in itself that they are working at cross-purposes to effectiveness?

For both creative people and their agencies, creative awards have a motivational capacity. They guide, often to a large extent, the kind of work agencies encourage

Some of the 3,000 commercial messages
researchers estimate we're exposed to each day

their clients to produce. Those clients often harbour scepticism and regard creativity as a distraction from selling. And it's perfectly reasonable to expect clients to require us to address that scepticism, to expect us to let creativity be such a driver only if we can prove that it's not a distraction from selling.

If indeed more creative advertising is less effective, then the case rests. Our industry has engineered itself to work hopelessly toward two mutually exclusive outcomes, and we need to rethink the way we're incentivised.

But if more creative advertising is more effective, then the creative awards system is, in a way, a beneficial incentive scheme – one that cunningly uses fame and peer cachet as a way to motivate agencies to produce more effective work for their clients.

Anecdotally, creative advertising does appear to punch above its weight.

According to the UK's Institute of Practitioners in Advertising, approximately one in every 7,000 campaigns is creative enough to win a creative award.[6] In other words, barely any advertising is highly creative.

Statistically speaking this means that effectiveness awards, which usually have in the vicinity of a few dozen awarded campaigns, should have either zero, or at very best one, creatively-awarded campaign among their ranks.

In fact, if you look at your local Effies show you'll find that usually around a fifth of the winners also received creative awards. Look at the remainder and you'll tend to find that most of those campaigns, while not being creative award material, are more creative than the average campaign you see on television. That's a massive over-representation of creative campaigns at effectiveness award shows, suggesting that more creative advertising does indeed work harder.

Of course, that is a very unscientific observation. And that's precisely the problem with the debate around creativity in advertising. It's based entirely on anecdotal evidence, piles of which exist on both sides of the debate.

Creative cynics will point to examples of creatively-awarded campaigns that haven't produced a business result, and to equally numerous examples of mega-brands being built on what could be described as uncreative marketing.

Those for creativity will use contrasting examples of creative award winners that have won major effectiveness accolades and point to highly creative challenger brands as evidence of the business potential of an original and colourful approach. Both sides seem to have a point. What's been lacking, however, is a conclusion. As passionate as both sides are in their rhetoric, and as convinced as they are by their own small sets of personal experience and anecdotal examples, neither has been capable of showing whether or not more creative advertising is, statistically speaking, more effective.

We typically net out at a circular game of conjecture. Our industry agrees to disagree. And we forge ahead in slightly different directions.

"So many creatives tell me, 'I wish we could prove that great ads actually made a difference'," says Tess

Alps, CEO of Thinkbox, the UK's marketing body for commercial broadcasters. "Creative awards are often derided by advertisers, who say, 'Oh it's just creative people awarding themselves at stupid self-indulgent ceremonies. It's got nothing to do with business'. Could we actually look at whether that was true or not? Is there a correlation between the sort of ads that gain awards and high levels of effectiveness?"[7] Alps was introducing the findings of a major study of creativity that we will look at later, but the question that she's asked is the very one this book hopes to answer.

If we are after more effective advertising, should we pursue a more creative approach, or a more conservative one?

And can we answer that question with something more sound than isolated examples and conjecture? Can we compare, with significant data sets and academic methodologies, the more creative agencies and campaigns with the less creative ones, and measure the effectiveness of those two groups?

Can we determine, once and for all, whether it is better for advertisers to employ a more creative agency and encourage a more creative approach? Is more creative advertising more effective advertising?

Let's find out.

The case for creative agencies

"Our objective is effectiveness. Our strategy is creativity."
— *Bartle Bogle Hegarty*

In 2006, *Advertising Age* marvelled at the $37 million they estimated Madison Avenue agencies would spend that year entering creative award programmes. "A number that looks like vanity gone wild," they said, "given that the pencils and lions are often denigrated as little more than ego-(and salary-)inflating devices for the creatives that crave them."[8]

The report went on to discover that the USA's six most creatively awarded agency networks – BBDO, DDB, TBWA, Ogilvy, Wieden+Kennedy and Saatchi & Saatchi – were also the fastest-growing, suggesting that creative awards might just be as attractive to clients as they are to creative people.

Despite that ostensible evidence, it's a suggestion that tends to be rejected. Judy Neer, president of Pile & Co (a consultancy that manages client/agency relationships) told *Advertising Age* that "our clients typically never care about award shows". Dick Roth, founder of similar company Roth Associates, agreed: "In making a new agency selection it is not a key criteria, at all … Does winning awards influence new business decisions? I think not."

Across the Atlantic, Martin Jones of UK relationship consultancy AAR told *Campaign* an illuminating story. "I was once asked to look at the customer journey that a new-business prospect might make when visiting a new agency," he said. "'What do clients think about putting creative awards up in reception?' was the first question. Unfortunately, the agency chief was expecting a definitive answer. My response had to take into account the way in which clients post-rationalise their thoughts: If they've had a good meeting and like the people, they will think you care about your product. If they've had a poor meeting, they will simply see your display of creative awards as being a focus on art rather than commerce."[9]

It's an insightful commentary on human nature, but also brings to light the issue that we are without general agreement on whether there is any correlation between creative awards and effectiveness, leaving clients' views of creative awards to be based solely on their feelings about the people who've won them.

That we choose to weigh creativity and effectiveness in separate baskets is a quirk that niggles even creative people.

"Everything that's wrong with the advertising business can be encapsulated by the fact that we have separate awards shows for creativity and effectiveness," said Deutsch L.A. Chief Creative Officer Eric Hirshberg to *Creativity* in 2008. "It's hard to imagine what the analogous award shows would be in other creative industries. It would be like the journalism industry giving out one award for prose, and another for *accuracy*."[10]

And yet as agreeable as Eric's words are, we are fortunate, in one sense at least, to have evolved in such a peculiar way. The oddity of separate measurement systems for creativity and effectiveness has afforded us the ability to learn whether there's truly a relationship between them.

By 2010, data from creative and effectiveness award programmes had become not only comprehensive but widely available. The Gunn Report provided a list of the world's 50 most creative agencies according to their performance at creative award shows. And the results of effectiveness shows such as the UK's IPA Effectiveness Awards and the USA's Effies were online for all to see. Nobody had compared the data sets at that point, but it didn't take more than a few quiet January mornings to punch them into a spreadsheet and see what happened.

I decided to use the data from a five-year period: 2006–2010, and looked at all the Gunn Report results and all the effectiveness awards won for those five years.

For my list of 'most creative' agencies, I wanted only the consistently creative shops, rather than agencies that had made it into the Gunn Report in one lucky year. So I made a list of those agencies that had been included in the Gunn Report's Top 50 at least twice between 2006 and 2010.

Then, to create a comparison 'less creative' group, I took major US and UK agencies who either hadn't made it into the Gunn Report Top 50, or had featured only once.

Some agencies choose not to enter effectiveness awards, and so to include them would confuse the data, as there's no way of telling how effective they would have been had they entered. So I included only agencies that had won at least one effectiveness award across the period – proof that they didn't have a policy against entering.

That left me with a group of twelve USA and six UK 'most creative' agencies, and a comparison group of twelve USA and six UK 'less creative' agencies:

Most Creative Agencies:	Less Creative Agencies:
Arnold (USA)	Campbell-Ewald (USA)
BBDO (USA)	Deutsch (USA)
BBH (USA)	Doner (USA)
Crispin Porter + Bogusky (USA)	DraftFCB (USA)
DDB (USA)	Euro RSCG (USA)
Goodby Silverstein & Partners (USA)	Grey (USA)
Grupo Gallegos (USA)	Hill Holliday (USA)
Leo Burnett (USA)	JWT (USA)
McCann Erickson (USA)	Ogilvy Advertising (USA)
Saatchi & Saatchi (USA)	Publicis (USA)
TBWA (USA)	Richards Group (USA)
Wieden+Kennedy (USA)	Y&R (USA)
AMV BBDO (UK)	JWT (UK)
BBH (UK)	M&C Saatchi (UK)
DDB (UK)	McCann Erickson (UK)
Fallon (UK)	Ogilvy Advertising (UK)
Leo Burnett (UK)	Publicis (UK)
Saatchi & Saatchi (UK)	RKCR/Y&R (UK)

Next, I tallied the effectiveness award wins from 2006–2010 for each agency. The USA tallies came from the North American Effie Awards and the UK tallies came from the UK's IPA Effectiveness Awards.

And a picture began to emerge.

The USA's most creative agencies averaged 13.3 Effies over the five-year period. The USA's less creative agencies averaged 8.2. The UK's most creative agencies averaged 4.7 IPA Effectiveness Awards over the five years (IPA awards being given out much more sparingly than Effies). The UK's less creative agencies averaged 4.0.

Overall, the most creative agencies had won 1.5 times as many effectiveness awards.

To bring more colour to the picture, I'd collected some extra data. I'd noted the quality of the effectiveness awards – i.e. whether they were a bronze, silver, gold, or 'Grand Effie' or 'IPA Grand Prix' – and then assigned a points system to those awards to show not only how many effectiveness awards an agency had won, but also the overall quality of those wins, giving each agency an 'effectiveness points' total for the period. A bronze earned one point, a silver two points, a gold three points and a grand four. This gave me a way to recognise the agencies that were truly the *most* effective.

With that data factored in, the most creative agencies proved even more effective – with an average of 1.7 times as many effectiveness points as their less creative counterparts.

Finally, I added in some financial information. Averaging revenue for the financial years 2005–2009 (the years when the work that was later awarded would have run), I found the most creative agencies to have been on average 10 per cent smaller than the less creative ones.

By dividing the revenue by the number of effectiveness awards, I could calculate the true measure of an agency's effectiveness – how *efficient* they'd been at achieving effectiveness – measured by how many effectiveness awards, and effectiveness points, they'd won per $100 million of revenue.

That data showed that the USA's most creative agencies won an average of 9.6 Effies, and 19.6 effectiveness points, per $100 million revenue. Their less creative

Effectiveness of 'Most Creative' and 'Less Creative' USA and UK Advertising Agencies 2006–2010

Most Creative Agencies:	Average Annual Revenue (US$)	Effectiveness Awards Won	Effectiveness Points	Effectiveness Awards Won / $100M Revenue	Effectiveness Points / $100M Revenue
McCann Erickson (USA)	469.7	7	13	1.5	2.8
BBDO (USA)	453.8	18	35	4.0	7.7
DDB (USA)	277.0	35	70	12.6	25.3
Leo Burnett (USA)	248.9	29	55	11.7	22.1
Saatchi & Saatchi (USA)	201.0	10	22	5.0	10.9
TBWA (USA)	192.9	12	28	6.2	14.5
Arnold (USA)	129.2	4	7	3.1	5.4
Crispin Porter + Bogusky (USA)	105.9	8	17	7.6	16.1
Weiden+Kennedy (USA)	91.6	10	20	10.9	21.8
Goodby Silverstein & Partners (USA)	85.4	19	45	22.2	52.7
BBH (USA)	32.4	6	14	18.5	43.2
Grupo Gallegos (USA)	8.1	1	1	12.4	12.4
AMV BBDO (UK)	57.3	6	14	10.5	24.4
BBH (UK)	33.9	12	24	35.4	70.9
Leo Burnett (UK)	27.1	3	7	11.1	25.9
DDB (UK)	26.4	4	7	15.2	26.6
Saatchi & Saatchi (UK)	24.8	1	2	4.0	8.1
Fallon (UK)	19.6	2	5	10.2	25.5
USA MOST CREATIVE AVERAGE	191.3	13.3	27.3	9.6	19.6
UK MOST CREATIVE AVERAGE	31.5	4.7	9.8	14.4	30.2
MOST CREATIVE AVERAGE	**138.1**	**10.4**	**21.4**	**11.2**	**23.1**

The 'Most Creative' agencies are those that have appeared in the Gunn Report Top 50 at least twice between 2006 and 2010

The 'Less Creative' agencies are large USA and UK agencies that won at least one Effectiveness Award between 2006 and 2010, and who either did not appear in the Gunn Report Top 50 between 2006 and 2010 or appeared only once.

'Average Annual Revenue' is average revenue 2005 - 2009, as reported in industry journals 'Advertising Age' (USA) and 'Campaign' (UK)

'Effectiveness Points' are calculated as follows: 1 point for a Bronze, 2 points for a Silver, 3 points for a Gold and 4 points for a Grand Effie or IPA Grand Prix

Less Creative Agencies:	Average Annual Revenue (US$)	Effectiveness Awards Won	Effectiveness Points	Effectiveness Awards Won / $100M Revenue	Effectiveness Points / $100M Revenue
JWT (USA)	348.9	25	45	7.2	12.9
DraftFCB (USA)	327.5	3	12	0.9	3.7
Y&R (USA)	278.8	5	10	1.8	3.6
Ogilvy Advertising (USA)	235.8	25	47	10.6	19.9
Euro RSCG (USA)	226.8	6	11	2.6	4.9
Grey (USA)	226.0	11	20	4.9	8.8
Campbell-Ewald (USA)	195.9	5	9	2.6	4.6
Publicis (USA)	173.7	5	8	2.9	4.6
Richards Group (USA)	162.1	2	5	1.2	3.1
Doner (USA)	157.8	3	7	1.9	4.4
Deutsch (USA)	147.6	7	13	4.7	8.8
Hill Holliday (USA)	138.9	1	2	0.7	1.4
JWT (UK)	42.1	4	7	9.5	16.6
McCann Erickson (UK)	41.0	3	4	7.3	9.8
M&C Saatchi (UK)	35.9	1	2	2.8	5.6
Rainey Kelly Campbell Roalfe/Y&R (UK)	33.1	10	22	30.2	66.5
Ogilvy Advertising (UK)	31.0	5	6	16.1	19.3
Publicis (UK)	30.8	1	1	3.2	3.2
USA LESS CREATIVE AVERAGE	218.3	8.2	15.8	3.5	6.7
UK LESS CREATIVE AVERAGE	35.7	4.0	7.0	11.5	20.2
LESS CREATIVE AVERAGE	**157.4**	**6.8**	**12.8**	**6.2**	**11.2**
THE MOST CREATIVE AGENCIES:	**0.9** Times as big	**1.5** Times as many Effectiveness Awards	**1.7** Times as many Effectiveness Points	**1.8** Times as many Effectiveness Awards per $1B	**2.1** Times as many Effectiveness Points per $1B

fellow Americans won just 3.5 Effies and 6.7 effectiveness points.

The UK's most creative agencies won an average of 14.4 IPA Effectiveness Awards, and 30.2 effectiveness points, per $100 million revenue. The less creative UK shops won just 11.5 IPA awards and 20.2 points.

What this revealed was that in terms of true overall effectiveness, the most creative shops were over twice as effective. They'd won 1.8 times as many effectiveness awards and 2.1 times as many effectiveness points.

In 2015 I was curious to see if the findings we published four years earlier still held true. The stars of the Gunn Report were still mostly shining. In fact, they'd become even more consistent, with agencies such as AMV BBDO and adam&eveDDB in the UK, and Wieden+Kennedy Portland and BBDO New York in the USA appearing every year in the report's top 50 between 2010 and 2014.

This allowed me to compare 12 'super-creative' agencies – shops that had been in the Gunn Report three or more times over that period – with 17 other agencies that appeared only once or twice. This would help establish whether highly creative agencies get *more* effective as they get more creative.

In the UK, I used the same points system. Four for an IPA Grand Prix, three for a gold, two for a silver and one for a bronze. The agencies that had appeared only once or twice in The Gunn Report averaged just over four points for the period. The super-creative agencies, by contrast, averaged nearly 18 points – more than three and a half times as much success at effectiveness awards.

In the US, I relied on the system now used by the Effie Index, the ranking system developed to showcase the most successful agencies at the global Effie Awards programmes. They give eight points to a gold, six to a silver and four to a bronze award. The findings were similar. The agencies that appeared only once or twice in The Gunn Report averaged a touch under 30 points for the period. The super-creative shops averaged more than two and a half times more, at nearly 79 points.

By punching in the available revenue figures for the US agencies and billing figures for the UK agencies we can see that again, the super-creative agencies were much more efficient at achieving their effectiveness awards. The super-creative US agencies' average of 60 effectiveness points for every $100M billed eclipsed the other agencies who managed just 27. Eerily, the ratio is identical in the UK. The super-creative UK agencies averaged six effectiveness points for every £100M billed against the other agencies' 2.7. In both markets, the super-creative agencies were 2.2 times as efficient as their less creative peers.

Creative ambition raises eyebrows not because the business world is against creativity per se, but rather because of the nervousness they feel that agencies will prioritise creativity over effectiveness. But is it really ever a case of prioritising one over the other?

BBH devised perhaps the most lucid explanation of the relationship between the two.

"Our objective is effectiveness," they say.

"Our strategy is creativity."

Super-Creative UK Agencies	Gun Report Top 50 Appearances 2010-2014	2014 Billings (£M)	IPA Effectiveness Award Points 2010-2014	Effectiveness Points per £100K Billed
AMV BBDO	5	468	28	6.0
Adam&EveDDB	5	259	15	5.8
BBH	3	221	15	6.8
RKCR/Y&R	3	239	13	5.4
SUPER-CREATIVE AVERAGE		297	17.75	6.0

Other Creative UK Agencies				
CHI & Partners	2	187	3	1.6
Mother	2	157	1	0.6
Ogilvy & Mather	2	126	5	4.0
Leo Burnett	1	201	8	4.0
M&C Saatchi	1	126	5	4.0
Saatchi & Saatchi	1	142	3	2.1
OTHER CREATIVE AVERAGE		157	4	2.7

Super-Creative US Agencies	Gun Report Top 50 Appearances 2010-2014	2014 Revenue ($M)	IPA Effectiveness Award Points 2011-2015	Effectiveness Points per $100K Revenue
BBDO	5	577	140	24.3
Wieden & Kennedy	5	183	124	67.8
BBH	4	37	56	151.4
Droga5	4	78	104	133.3
Leo Burnett	3	487	170	34.9
R/GA	3	258	9	3.5
TBWA	3	331	28	8.5
SUPER-CREATIVE AVERAGE		297	90	60.5

Other Creative US Agencies				
Creative Artists Agency	2	647	18	2.8
DDB	2	288	29	10.1
Deutsch	2	188	16	8.5
Goodby Silverstein & Partners	2	109	41	37.6
Arnold Worldwide	1	95	50	52.6
Grey	1	318	80	25.2
JWT	1	435	30	6.9
Periera & Odell	1	24	14	58.3
The Martin Agency	1	121	31	25.6
Venables Bell & Partners	1	39	18	46.2
OTHER CREATIVE AVERAGE		226	33	27.4

Super-creative UK agencies won 2.2 times as many effectiveness points per £100K of billings as other creative UK agencies

Super-creative US agencies won 2.2 times as many effectiveness points per $100K of revenue as other creative US agencies

The 'Super-Creative' agencies are those that have appeared in the Gunn Report Top 50 more than 3 times between 2010 and 2014

The 'Other Creative' agencies are those that have appeared in the Gunn Report Top 50 once or twice between 2010 and 2014

'Billings' and 'Revenue' information is as reported in industry journals 'Advertising Age' (USA) and 'Campaign' (UK)

'Effectiveness Points' are calculated as follows: UK: 1 point for a Bronze, 2 points for a Silver, 3 points for a Gold and 4 points for an IPA Grand Prix; US: 4 points for a Bronze, 6 points for a Silver, 8 points for a Gold.

At a guess I'd say their mantra resonates with creatively ambitious agencies everywhere. Rather than a case of one or the other being most important, creativity is simply the strategy to achieve effectiveness.

The numbers suggest that's working – which is unsurprising given business history has shown that the companies that truly live and breathe their strategies are the ones that most often achieve their objectives.

There is clearly a lot more to choosing an agency than simply checking how many awards they've won – and of course, within these studies, there exists a small handful of extremely effective agencies that have gone without at creative award shows.

However, what these findings suggest is that, by and large, if an agency does well at creative award shows, it'll also be doing well in terms of effectiveness; that there is a much stronger correlation between high creativity and high effectiveness than there is between lower creativity and high effectiveness; and that if you see a ridiculous surfeit of pencils and lions in the reception area of an agency you're visiting, it's probably evidence of something more than just creativity.

A popular execution from Honda's *Power of Dreams* campaign

Identifying creativity

"Creativity is whatever isn't something else."

— *Peter Shillingsburg, Author and Academic*

"Oh, blimey," Jeremy Bullmore once said about creativity. "Clients know they want it; agencies know they've got to deliver it; but nobody knows what it is."[11]

So before we go too much further, it might be useful to pause for a moment and define what we mean by 'creativity'. What exactly is 'creative' advertising and how does it differ from the uncreative?

"Creativity is extremely difficult to define," says David Lubars, "but incredibly easy to identify."

David is Chairman and Chief Creative Officer of BBDO, for many years the most creatively awarded advertising network in the world.[12] Which gives us some idea of how far up the food chain creativity's famed undefinability persists.

Bill Bernbach was quick to warn against worrying too much about it. "It's like love," he said of creativity. "The more you analyse it, the faster it disappears."

Even so, it would be somewhat uncooperative to present the case for creativity while refusing to explain what we mean by 'creative' advertising. And, as David suggests, though we might not define creativity, there are a handful of things that, in the eyes of the most creative advertising and marketing people, easily identify the truly creative campaigns in advertising's pack.

Peter Shillingsburg, a Professor or English, once said that "creativity is whatever isn't something else", echoing the commonly-held belief that creativity is most easily identified when something new is brought into existence out of nothing. Originality is the first and perhaps most unambiguous characteristic of creativity. Well-trodden territory is easily identified, and recycled ideas are unceremoniously disregarded by creative award judges.

"Great work should make you feel uncomfortable because it hasn't been done before," says Tony Davidson, Executive Creative Director of Wieden+ Kennedy London. His agency, one of the most respected in the world for its creativity, is famous for legendary campaigns such as Nike's 'Run London' and Honda's 'Power of Dreams'. Speaking of the less creative pitches that occasionally slip, Tony says, "Ken Keir, head of Honda Europe, still to this day looks us in the eye and says 'it's not making me feel uncomfortable'. More brave clients like him please."

"To me, more creative marketing takes a really big step," says Jim McDowell, former President of Mini USA, and Chief Marketing Officer of BMW during the period of their winning Cannes Advertiser of the Year. "It's not a small incremental add-on to something you've seen before. It takes a really big step in a direction that I'd never even imagined. From that perspective you go 'oh wow, that truly is amazing and I wish I'd have thought of that myself'. That's the way it works in my mind."

The second characteristic of creative campaigns is probably best described as 'engagement'. The ability of an idea not only to communicate clearly, but also to be so interesting or enjoyable to engage with that people freely choose to spend time with it.

"The area which probably comes to mind when someone talks about 'creativity'," say researchers from Millward Brown, "is the big executional creative idea; the powerful or emotionally appealing creative hook, introduced to communicate more effectively."[13]

Uncreative work tends to start with a conviction that we simply need to clearly and comprehensively deliver marketing information, and that if we can do that in a way that's enjoyable to the consumer then that's 'nice to have', but not fundamentally necessary. That conviction stems from a belief that people naturally pay attention to, and consume, all the advertising that is put in front of them. That media in itself creates a willing audience for the message.

Conversely, the most creative work starts with the contrary belief that people naturally block out advertising and only consume the small amount of advertising that captures their interest. Media in itself makes an audience a possibility, but not a certainty – a thousand people passing by a billboard is not an audience of a thousand people. The true audience number is the number of people that actually notice and engage with the billboard, and that the quality of the idea determines the size of that audience.

The most creative work comes from a conviction that first we need to surprise and engage people, and to do so in a way that allows us to credibly and relevantly follow through with a marketing message.

"I think that first it has to touch something in me that makes me care," says Jim Stengel, former P&G Global Marketing Officer. "After we went to Cannes for the first time back in 2003, we decided that we were going to start measuring whether consumers told us 'I want to see that again'. And I think if people say that it touches them and makes them care, and they want to see it again, I think those are two very powerful ideas."

Saatchi & Saatchi's UK Director of Strategy, Richard Huntington, refers to this care factor as 'interestingness'. "Strategists spend vast swathes of time desperately trying to be right, with the result that the majority of strategic thinking is clichéd, lame and dreary."

His advice is to start by worrying about being interesting. "I guess my professional mantra of late has been summed up in the phrase 'it is vital to be interesting, it is merely important to be right'."[14]

"Then there is the execution," says Nick Worthington, Creative Chairman at New Zealand's Colenso BBDO. "What all great campaigns have in common is a great idea and great execution. If the head is seduced by 'the idea' then the heart is almost certainly won over by the execution."

Great 'craft' is the third characteristic of creatively superior work. Creative people tend to support the belief that any idea, no matter how good, has the potential to be anything from dismal failure to runaway success, and that the defining factor is its execution – those things like choice of music, art direction, or quality of photography.

"Ideas are just a multiplier of execution," agrees entrepreneur Derek Sivers. "To me, ideas are worth nothing unless executed. They are just a multiplier. Execution is worth millions."

Derek, the seminal online retailer tech millionaire who founded CD Baby, uses a chart to explain:

Awful idea	−1	No execution	$1
Weak idea	1	Weak execution	$1,000
So-so idea	5	So-so execution	$10,000
Good idea	10	Good execution	$100,000
Great idea	15	Great execution	$1,000,000
Brilliant idea	20	Brilliant execution	$10,000,000

"You need to multiply the two," he says. "The most brilliant idea, with no execution, is worth $20. The most brilliant idea takes great execution to be worth $20,000,000."[15]

Though we talk a lot about ideas in advertising, in fact what contributes to the creative quality, and ultimately the effectiveness of advertising, is as much to do with its execution. As BBH's John Hegarty is credited with saying, "a great ad is 80 per cent idea and 80 per cent execution".[16]

"At Leo Burnett we developed a 10-point scale to look at work in a conceptual way," says Michael Conrad, formerly Leo Burnett's Chief Creative Officer and now President of the Berlin School of Creative Leadership. "Called '7plus', it eliminated vague judgement and argumentation. We used 7plus to evaluate progress every three months by running a meeting looking at 1,000 to 1,200 pieces of work from all over the network. It did not take long until this practice moved from 'post' to 'pre'. You could call it 'Total Quality Management' in the ideas business. Within the first five years of 7plus, 27 Leo Burnett agencies were named Agency of the Year in their countries at least once."

The 7plus scale was made up of 10 categories, divided into three sections:

10	Most Inspiring in the World
9	New Standard in Communication
8	New Standard in Category
7	Excellence in Craft
6	Fresh Idea(s)
5	Innovative Strategy
4	Cliché
3	Non Competitive
2	Destructive
1	Appalling

"[From] 1 to 4 is what we wanted to avoid," says Michael. "8 to 10 is where we wanted to be. And 5 to 7 are qualities you need to have in order to avoid inferior work or to lay the tracks to superior work."

As well as helping identify the most creative work, the 7plus scale suggests something of a definition of uncreative work. In between the creative campaigns and those advertisements so poor as to be labelled 'appalling' or 'destructive' are campaigns that Michael and his team labelled 'non-competitive' and 'cliché'.

Saying the same thing as the other guy, or saying something that the consumer has heard time and time again, is the first sure sign of uncreativity. Fortunately, as tempting as it can sometimes be to make worn-out, non-competitive claims such as having the tastiest taste or producing the whitest whites, the idea of differentiation has largely been ingrained into the canon of accepted marketing wisdom.

However, encouragement to use clichéd executional ideas is more pervasive. In the mid-2000s, after being slapped on the hand for their highly original (and sometimes regulation-defying) advertising, New Zealand vodka brand 42Below produced the following radio announcement:

"Due to the regulations surrounding New Zealand alcohol advertising, all our future ads will be about three 'mates' in their mid to late twenties on a quest to find 'a good time'. This quest will involve them in various 'shenanigans' until they finally find satisfaction by discovering 42Below Vodka at some unexpected tavern.

These 'mates' must be average white males, one of whom must seem a bit 'goofy'. 42Below will investigate the possibility of a token Maori mate appearing from time to time. New Zealand alcohol advertising regulations also stress that the three 'mates' will at some stage associate with three white females in denim shorts or bikinis, to show that they are not poofs. However, these women should not in any way distract them from completing their initial quest, which is to find 42Below Vodka. The advert will contain three gags, and I say 'gags', every fifteen seconds, contemporary rock music and at least one scene in an old Holden, cleverly written so it doesn't imply drink driving of any sort. We trust you'll find these new 42Below Vodka ads frickin' hilarious."

Although we make fun of the clichés, how often do we still seek refuge in the ultra-familiar? It's comforting to believe that formulaic advertising scenarios, albeit unexciting, won't risk being misunderstood or alienating groups of consumers. And yet how often do we need to see people offended by the clichés? "Do those companies think we're idiots or what?"

Four decades earlier, Leo Burnett himself had attempted a definition of creativity. It is, he said, "the art of establishing new and meaningful relationships between previously unrelated things in a manner that is relevant, believable, and in good taste, but which somehow presents the product in a fresh new light".

His words reflect a caution that creative leaders are often quick to impress on us. That, unlike the fields of art and entertainment, advertising isn't just about producing original, engaging and well-crafted ideas; and that the real trick of advertising is doing so in a way that solves the problem of selling a client's product.

James McGrath is Creative Chairman of Australia's Clemenger BBDO advertising network, one of his country's most awarded networks in terms of both creativity and effectiveness. James' criteria for judging creative awards go beyond the artistic merits of the work.

"What great award-worthy and effective campaigns have that others don't would have to be their ability to make an extraordinary idea work only because of the vital inclusion of the product. In judging terms it's the foundation on which you begin to then take all the subsequent conceptual, intellectual and executional elements into account. From there it's a matter of relevance. Sure, an idea might be doing it like it's never been done before, but if it's a simple, vain and self-conscious affectation disconnected from the product, an insight, or most importantly the consumer, then it's nothing more than a self-serving exercise."

"My favourite creative work," agrees Tony Davidson, "makes me wonder 'how did they come up with that', and yet at the same time feel it is really right for that brand. That is a real skill. I guess in my work, I've always asked the question: 'why is that right for this brand?' You often see award-winning work which is just a sponsored joke that does little for the brand. Most of the best work I have been involved in has a deep insight or truth that has been uncovered by digging deep into the company or product. Advertising making stuff up feels wrong. That's why I am still really proud of work like 'Run London' that we launched 10 years ago and was a 360°, integrated experience that tied back into product. And all of the great Honda work we have done comes from true insights."

In the 1990s, Donald Gunn produced his landmark study 'Do Award-winning Commercials Sell?' in which he showed that over 80 per cent of awarded advertising had met or exceeded its client's objectives. We'll cover the study in detail later, but among Donald's conclusions is the advice that for creativity to be effective, it needs to be an amplifier of sound strategic thinking, rather than a replacement for it.

"The evidence is overwhelming," he says, "well-focused commercials, which are based on the right message and, in addition, deliver it and translate it freshly, charmingly, engagingly and intelligently work better than commercials with the right message but which lack these creative qualities."

As Ernest Hemingway advised, "the most essential gift for a good writer is a built-in, shockproof, shit detector". The very best creative people seem to know not only how to be creative – how to find an innovative point of view, wrap it up in a fresh and engaging executional idea and then execute it with a high degree of craft quality – but importantly how to use creativity to solve problems and sell products. To create things of real value, rather than shit.

And so, in the interests of not analysing it until it disappears, that's probably what we mean by 'creativity'.

The case for originality

"We are not here to do what has already been done."

— *Robert Henri, American painter*

In 2005, in Auckland, a group called Godmarks launched a campaign of billboards designed to generate a more positive feeling toward Christianity. White words on a black background from He Himself said things like, "I was just thinking about you", "I love everyone, even Christians", and, my own favourite, "Well, you did ask for a sign".

At an end-of-year gathering, filled with the spirit of Christmas, I dared to speak some kind words about the campaign among a group of creative people.

The group hastened to recalibrate my view, pointing out that the campaign was a copy of an earlier American campaign, and in light of this poverty of originality, was utterly meritless.

An idealistic judgement, one might say. Regardless of whether or not the campaign was effective, it was no good because it wasn't 'original'. The evening wasn't spoiled with an argument, but the question had been asked: why do we have such an obsession with originality?

We all know it's true. An unoriginal idea, no matter how engaging or strategically sound, will struggle to make it out of most creative departments. The words 'it's been done' will fell the biggest of ideas in the coldest of blood.

The Godmarks campaign had proven effective in the USA, and was employed in New Zealand because of its prior performance. Yet the belief persisted that it would have been more virtuous to have created a purely original campaign, never mind that it might not have served Godmarks so well.

That conviction is both staunch and widespread. But the reasons for it are less apparent. Why do we advertising people have such an inhospitable response to the unoriginal?

Four years later at Colenso BBDO, halfway through a pre-production meeting to finalise details of the filming of a new campaign for our Vodafone client, our account director passed around a phone playing a YouTube clip he'd been sent.

We were well past the point of no return on what we were sure was an original idea – staging a performance of Tchaikovsky's *1812 Overture* using the text alert sounds of a thousand mobile phones.[18] So our discovery of a similar film showing a performance of jingle bells using the 'ding' sounds of 49 microwaves was disconcerting.[19] We were innocent of any imitation, but we weren't certain others would see it that way.

It's only human to feel a sense of injustice when we learn of those who've knowingly passed off others' work

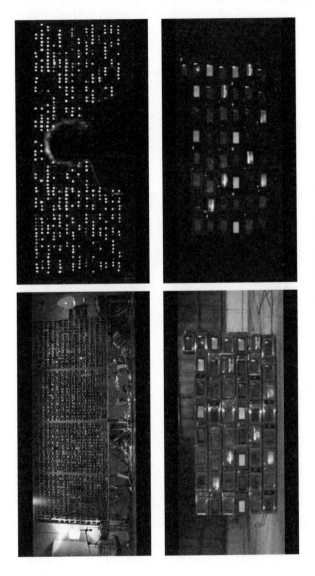

Vodafone's *Symphonia* (top); AKQA's Christmas video

as their own. Blogs at home and abroad are rife with accusatory posts spotlighting copycat advertising. Some of them are no doubt accurate – but being falsely accused is one of creativity's most common professional hazards.

There's almost as much damage in being accused of plagiarism as there is in plagiarism itself. Innocence is difficult to prove. "What are the chances!" you joke. And that's precisely what everybody else is thinking. What are the chances?

Two people conjuring up the same idea at the same time is regarded as highly suspicious. It seems a thoroughly improbable occurrence. It may be conceivable that two different people could have similar ideas, but at the same time? And yet, surprisingly, it turns out to be entirely common.

In his *New Yorker* essay 'In The Air: Who Says Big Ideas Are Rare?', Malcolm Gladwell touches on the work of William Ogburn and Dorothy Thomas, who in 1922 created a surprisingly long list of major ideas that had been simultaneously had by different scientists and inventors.[20]

Frenchmen Charles Cros and Louis Ducos du Hauron both invented colour photography at the same time in the mid-nineteenth century. In 1608, the telescope was independently invented by Hans Lippershey, Zacharias Janssen and Jacob Metius. The thermometer is claimed by at least six different men. And historians estimate the typewriter was created in the eighteenth century, by separate inventors, 52 times across Europe and America.

These occurrences of multiple discovery turned out

to be anything but rare. Ogburn and Thomas found 148 major examples of such multiplicity.

Evolution, so commonly attributed to Charles Darwin, was also discovered by Alfred Russel Wallace. Calculus was invented by both Isaac Newton and Gottfried Wilhelm Leibniz. The telegraph was pioneered simultaneously in 1837 by the Englishman Charles Wheatstone and the American Samuel Morse. And both the steamboat and the jet engine were designed by several independent engineers in the eighteenth and twentieth centuries, respectively.

In the 1960s, American sociologist Robert Merton furthered the study of multiplicity, concluding that "the pages of the history of science record thousands of instances of similar discoveries having been made by scientists working independently of one another. Sometimes the discoveries are simultaneous or almost so; sometimes a scientist will make a new discovery which, unknown to him, somebody else had made years before."

The title of Gladwell's essay spoke to the theory that ideas, rather than being born in the minds of their creators, are in fact 'in the air', to be discovered by anybody searching in the right direction at that particular moment. The sentiment reflects the words of Hungarian mathematician Farkas Bolyai, who in the nineteenth century suggested that "when the time is ripe for certain things, these things appear in different places in the manner of violets coming to light in early spring."

In 2003, Dan Futterman finished his screenplay

Capote within weeks of fellow biographer Douglas McGrath submitting *Infamous*. The writers, completely unknown to each other, had chosen not only the same subject, but also exactly the same period of Truman Capote's life. The history of film-making records dozens of such examples. *The Truman Show* (1998) and *EdTV* (1999) share an identical premise, as do *Deep Impact* and *Armageddon* (both 1998). *Groundhog Day* (1993) had a twin in *12:01*, a TV movie of the same year. *Lambada* was released on the same day in 1990 as *The Forbidden Dance*, also about the Lambada dance craze. *Turner & Hooch* and *K-9*, both about a police officer getting a dog for a partner, were released simultaneously in 1989. The novel *Les Liaisons Dangereuses* was adapted as *Dangerous Liaisons* in 1988 and *Valmont* in 1989. More recently, *Coco Before Chanel* and *Coco Chanel & Igor Stravinsky* were independently released within weeks of each other.

American writer Charles Fort also appeared to believe that ideas were 'in the air'. Trying to explain the six or seven inventions of the steam engine within a three-month window, saying "I guess it was just steam engine time". That designation – 'steam engine time' – has since been used by some to describe those cases of a single idea appearing at once in several unconnected minds.

How fascinating a notion, that external conditions at specific times create an environment in which certain ideas become 'likely'.

And yet the theory offered scant solace for those of us working on the Vodafone campaign. Our fears of being gleefully exposed and unsympathetically trialled were not without good cause.

Copying somebody else's idea is creativity's most detestable of sins. It's cheating. It's scandalous. And in our highly competitive field, it's just the sort of thing that our contemporaries hope we've been up to.

So much so that perhaps originality has become a self-preservation mechanism. Maybe our single-minded pursuit of originality is simply the surest way to keep our reputation untainted.

Or could it be because originality of thought is a romantic trait – a mark displayed by artists and scientists – of the sort of genius we covet for ourselves?

Advertising has occasional parallels with the art world, and most modern artists are as obsessed with originality as we are.

This has not always been the case. Our modern notion that the artist's work must be original would have been completely foreign to the Egyptian, Chinese or Byzantine master.

Up until the end of the Renaissance, an artist who deliberately sought originality would have been considered mad rather than gifted. A great artist used to be a copyist – of the ancients, of nature, of the ideal form.

What Michelangelo did with *David*, the Greek sculptor Praxiteles had done 18 centuries earlier with *Hermes*. Vermeer's *The Girl with the Pearl Earring* was often called the '*Mona Lisa* of the North' for its similarities to Leonardo's masterpiece. It wasn't a term of derision, rather a mark of respect for an artist who'd managed to replicate so successfully the effect of another master. Not until the eighteenth century were unpredictability and eccentricity seen as signs of genius.

David (left); Hermes

The same goes for literature. Rather than writing original plays, Shakespeare appropriated sources and fashioned them anew, whereas modern writers are sensitive to any similarity of plot or prose. "Originality – not just innocence of plagiarism but the making of something really and truly new – set itself down as a cardinal literary virtue sometime in the middle of the eighteenth century and has never since gotten up," says literary critic Thomas Mallon.

Today, originality is the yardstick against which most art is measured. American painter Robert Henri captured the artist's pursuit in 1923: "We are not here to do what has already been done."

In its 31 December 1999 issue, *Time* magazine revealed its list of the 100 most important people of the twentieth century. At the top was Albert Einstein. The embodiment of scientific genius, Einstein's originality of thought is stupefying. Even those of genius themselves were perplexed by the notion of relativity. Nobel Prize-winning physicist Richard Feynman famously commented, "I still can't see how he thought of it".

Despite Einstein's genius, *Time*'s choice to sit him atop its list was an interesting one. To people who think for a living, like other scientists, artists or even advertising creatives, Einstein is relevant. He was the ultimate thinker. He developed an understanding of relativity *just by thinking about it*. But to the rest of the world – the much larger group who don't spend their days in labs and studios – the great physicist's relevance is limited. One could argue that Martin Luther King's struggle for racial equality has had a greater impact on our everyday lives; that Churchill's tenacity in the face of fascism saved democracy; that Ford's vision of the motorcar changed everything; and that for their direct and tangible influence on all of our lives, one of them should take precedence over any theoretical scientist.

So why the kudos for Einstein, a man most famous for thinking up something that most of us don't even understand? Perhaps the answer lies in the fact that the twentieth century was characterised by an obsession with original thinking. We evolved from a culture that rewarded conformity and tradition to one that celebrated individuality and innovation. This democracy of thought is what many would consider the greatest cultural shift of the twentieth century.

Within this context, original thinking has become loved and revered – both as a symbol of freedom and an agent of progress. Those we believe to be geniuses we hold in the esteem that earlier generations reserved for royalty. Albert Einstein is King. Creative people can hardly be blamed for striving toward originality. Society worships it.

But what role does originality play in advertising effectiveness? It's all very well to value originality in and of itself, but as Mark Twain said, "the man with a new idea is a crank until the idea succeeds".

When Bill Bernbach observed that "you cannot sell to a man who isn't listening", he was inferring that more original advertising was more likely to capture attention. That originality was the key to making your campaign one of the few that didn't go unnoticed. He was proven right when, half a century later, five groups of university academics from the USA and Europe studied the effects of originality. They all found that the more original ads were more likely to stand out and be noticed.[21]

But does originality do more than merely make campaigns stand out? Does it, for example, enhance the appeal of creative work?

An analysis of successful creativity in the entertainment industry draws a frustrating conclusion: the more original the product, the less it seems to appeal to most people.

It's easy to cringe at the success of the Backstreet Boys. Poster boys for a generation of derivative, formulaic, highly engineered pop, they have sold a staggering 130 million albums globally, including 32 million copies of their eponymous 1995 debut.

Contrast them with one of their most lauded, influential and original peers: Radiohead. Considered by many critics to be among the greatest albums of all time, *OK Computer* has appeared at or near the top of virtually every major 'best albums' list, from *Rolling Stone* to the *Guardian*. And yet this masterpiece has sold only 8 million copies worldwide. It's difficult to see the justice in the Backstreet Boys' debut album outselling one of the most original creative efforts of the twentieth century by a factor of four.

Björk, one of the most innovative and fearless songwriters of all time, had sold around 10 million albums by the time Dido released her debut *No Angel*. Despite one critic describing the record as "music to microwave lasagne to", it sold 13 million copies, dwarfing Bjork's entire career in 52 minutes flat.

The box office paints a similar picture. As at 2015, 50 films from history had grossed over US$800 million globally.[22] 28 were film adaptations of popular books or comics (such as the *Harry Potter* and *Avengers* franchises) or historical stories *(Titanic)*. 16 were sequels in previously successful franchises *(Jurassic World, Furious 7)*. Just six films were original from their conception. And even those big hitters, including *Avatar*, *The Lion King* and *Independence Day*, all follow the formulaic three-act linear structure that Hollywood demands.

When screenwriters pen a film that they hope will be made in Los Angeles, they're required to follow a prescriptive set of rules that determine the length and structure of the film. The fact is that Hollywood leaves very little room for originality because most people tend not to enjoy original films. Sure, films such as Cannes Palme d'Or winners *Pulp Fiction* and *Fahrenheit 911* and popular classics *Forrest Gump* and *ET* have met with both critical acclaim and enormous box office success, but the rule prevails – if we're looking to entertain a mass audience, we're better to show them something they're familiar with.

But what if, rather than to entertain, we want to persuade an audience? Is originality more helpful than familiarity when forming an argument?

At Ogilvy London in 2004, planner Olivia Johnson was conducting research for her client, Dove, with the aid of feminist icons such as Susie Orbach and Gloria Steinem. The resulting report, 'The Real Truth About Beauty', showed that just nine per cent of women considered themselves 'attractive', 60 per cent strongly agreed that 'society expects women to enhance their physical attractiveness' and 68 per cent strongly agreed that 'the media and advertising set an unrealistic standard of beauty that most women can never achieve'.[23]

Olivia responded with a strategy to question the image of beauty as defined and pumped out by the beauty industry. And so the Dove 'Campaign for Real Beauty' was born.[a] Well, almost.

The senior managers at Dove were predominantly male. They'd built a massive global business partly through advertising which, like all their cosmetic industry peers, used aspirational images of beautiful women. To suggest to them that they should shoulder the weight of an entire culture's manipulation and crusade philanthropically against it could easily have been dismissed as preposterous.

To give the strategy hope, one of Olivia's colleagues conceived of a highly original way to convince Dove of Olivia's thinking. They found the daughters of those mostly male senior managers. They filmed them talking candidly about how imperfect the images in the media made them feel. Then, at the creative presentation to Dove, they showed those tapes to their fathers.

It was a powerful argument. Businessmen are used to making rational, objective judgements, after taking in research presentations full of graphs and charts. An

---

a   Over the years I've heard several people conjecture that Dove's Campaign for Real Beauty was ineffective from a product sales point of view. It's worth noting that the campaign won effectiveness awards in the UK, USA and Canada, and that all three effectiveness case studies (all of which are available in the public domain) were based on product sales growth rather than simply brand or communications measures.

appeal from your own daughter is completely original. The campaign was approved and rolled out globally.

But would the outcome have been different if, in the weeks leading up to Olivia's presentation, other suppliers had pitched to those men, using video of their families to make the point?

Social psychologists in the late 1970s found that as people were repeatedly exposed to a 'persuasive message', they developed 'counterarguments', reducing their agreement with, and thus the persuasiveness of, the original argument.[24] That, over time, we develop a kind of 'immunity' to being 'sold to' with arguments we've seen or heard before.

Our psychological reaction to arguments is similar to our physical reaction to viruses. Our immune system, the first time it's exposed to a foreign body, has a tricky time beating it. However, when the virus returns, it's innocuous. We have no trouble dealing with an unoriginal virus. Likewise, an unoriginal argument is likely to suffer defeat at the hands of our cognitive immune system. There's an ability in all of us to think our way out of even the most robust argument given enough time.

A fresh argument, however, has the opportunity to make it through the mind's defences before they have time to beat it.

In 2008 marketing professors at Indiana University found this to hold true in practice. Testing advertising of varying levels of originality, they found that more original ads not only attracted more attention, but also reduced consumers' resistance to persuasion. "This is an important finding," they said, "because any strat-

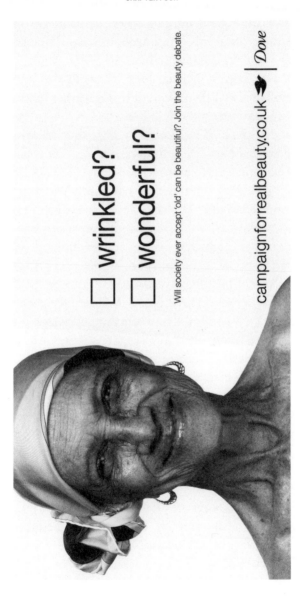

□ wrinkled?
□ wonderful?

Will society ever accept 'old' can be beautiful? Join the beauty debate.

campaignforrealbeauty.co.uk 🕊 | *Dove*

67

egy that can reduce resistance to persuasion and make consumers more open-minded can have a significant impact on brand purchase intentions."[25]

The ability of original ideas to stand out and be remembered is difficult to refute, but further to merely getting noticed, an original argument has a better chance of persuading people because they haven't yet developed cognitive immunity to it.

The nineteenth-century historian Thomas Carlyle said "originality is a thing we constantly clamour for, and constantly quarrel with". He was speaking in and of the Victorian era, but the sentiment rings true today. We clamour for originality and it's rewarded handsomely on the stages of our award shows, but in boardrooms and strategy meetings we constantly quarrel with it. What makes an original piece of communication, for example, a better bet than replicating something that we can see has worked in the past? Are we sure we're not being creative just for the sake of it?

Well, originality has been proven to aid in cut-through and persuasion. It's been proven to make communication more effective. But it also moves us forward. Keeping the muscle of originality well toned means we continually find new ways to engage with consumers, new ways to keep advertising palatable to society and new ways to differentiate products and brands. As another of *Time*'s 100 most important people, Coco Chanel, said: "In order to be irreplaceable one must always be different."

I'm with her.

Brady Bunch — one of the many creatively awarded executions from Snickers'
You're Not You When You're Hungry campaign, the only campaign in history to
have won two Cannes Creative Effectiveness Lions as well as golds at both the
UK's IPA Effectiveness Awards and the US Effies.

The case for creative advertising

"The extent to which they turned out to be more effective than non-creatively-awarded campaigns still remains astonishing to me."

— Peter Field, Author and Marketing Consultant

"In our business there is a substantial body of opinion that is dismissive if not scornful about creative awards. These industry colleagues – and they exist both at clients and in agencies – take the view that awards are basically a frivolity, and are wholly irrelevant, indeed probably counterproductive, to the main business in hand – the selling of products and services."[26]

These, in 1996, were the words of a troubled Donald Gunn, then working at one of the world's most creatively-awarded agencies.

"They assume and believe and also will broadcast the view that winning awards and selling products are, for the most part, and in some fundamental way, mutually exclusive. They clearly suspect that the motives that go into an ad that wins awards and an ad that is designed to sell are different. This makes a mockery of the value creative people place upon awards, which to them represent the highest recognition by their peers."

This rift eventually unsettled Donald to the point of action. "At Leo Burnett," he remembers, "I was the impetuous volunteer who conceived of, then carried out, the 'Do Award-winning Commercials Sell?' study. This consisted of identifying the 400 most-awarded commercials and campaigns in the world from 1992–1995, then painstakingly gathering in the 400 case histories."

The basic objective of his study was simple: to find out, once and for all, whether that commonly held cynicism about creative awards was right or wrong.

To analyse such a large pool of campaigns, Donald and his team reviewed the work of 129 agencies in 26 countries, arriving at a set of campaigns that had between them won 1,483 major creative awards.

Causing what must have been a record quarter in agency telecommunications costs, they called the CEO or Executive Creative Director of all 129 agencies, introduced the study and followed up with a simple questionnaire requesting the objectives and results of each campaign. If it had met or exceeded objectives, they required quantified evidence. If it hadn't, they asked why not.

"The result was pretty compelling," Donald recalls. "86.5 per cent of them had been associated with marketplace success." 336 of those 400 campaigns had met or exceeded the objectives set by their clients.

Of course, that left 54 underachievers. "A number of the cases failed to achieve objectives and to move business ahead. There were also four cases in the category 'Client considers successful, but no quantified data are available'. We counted these as No's."

The remaining huge majority were examples of effective advertising. Some of them modestly so, but "at the top end of the study was a group of cases – more than 100 of them, over 25 per cent of the total – where the level of business success was not just good, not just very good, but could more appropriately be described as amazing. Way beyond any increase you'd see written down in even the most aggressive marketing plan."

An emphatic result, but how accurate was this data? Would agencies have told Donald and his team if the advertising hadn't worked?

"Firstly," says Donald, "I was dealing on a confidential basis with very senior people at the world's best advertising agencies. And note that 54 of them did tell me that the advertising hadn't worked. My own belief is that good advertising people at this level are more interested in getting at the truth than in being proved personally right. Secondly, for 56 of the cases (all potential candidates to participate in the resulting presentation at the 1996 Cannes Lions Advertising Festival), I went back to the agencies for clearance to use the results and detailed numbers they'd provided. So they now knew that their data were liable to be quoted before 2,000 or so delegates at Cannes, including people from their own market or with intimate knowledge of their category. There was not a single case in the 56 where anyone back-tracked on their claims or wanted to downsize any numbers."

Donald and his colleagues at Leo Burnett felt the result was conclusive. "Which may suggest," they said, "that award show judges and our clients' customers have a whole lot in common in the way they react to advertising."

"But 1996," Donald admitted in 2010, "is a long time ago."

Three years after the conclusion of his landmark study, Donald ended three decades at Leo Burnett to launch his inaugural Gunn Report. The report is based, he says, "on a very simple idea. It combines the winners lists from all the major advertising award contests in the world to establish the annual worldwide league tables for the advertising industry.

"Totting up award shows for a living might seem like a somewhat frivolous endeavour," he admitted at a recent UK conference, "but it has a serious underpinning. For I devoutly believe in the power of creativity to produce sales for the immediate present at the same time as it builds reputation for the long haul."

The Gunn Report's raison d'être is to rank agencies and campaigns according to their creativity. It has nothing to do with effectiveness. But, inadvertently, it had grown into a set of data that would prove invaluable in the *study* of effectiveness.

"It's something I'd been thinking about for years," says UK marketing consultant Peter Field. "A few years ago I heard Donald Gunn give his presentation on creativity. It occurred to me that he had this fantastic database of creativity, and I had my hands on a rather handy database of effectiveness."

Peter, an independent contractor to the UK's Institute of Practitioners in Advertising, was for the second time mining the IPA Effectiveness Databank case studies to help the IPA and their member agencies understand what led to more effective advertising.

"Donald spoke very academically about creativity and that's a rare commodity – somebody who obviously has his finger very firmly on the creative pulse, but can also put a presentation together and do a bit of number crunching. It took me about three years to get it off the ground, but when I put the proposal to Donald he leapt at it."

His proposal to Donald was to fuse the Gunn report database of creatively-awarded campaigns with the IPA Effectiveness Databank to examine the link between creativity and effectiveness.

"Increasingly I think the climate is more toward understanding the benefits of creative awards," observes Peter. "P&G have had a famous conversion on this – from 15 or 20 years ago forbidding any of their agencies from even entering creative awards to now pitching up at Cannes every year feeling that they can learn from that. So there have been some very conspicuous client conversions to the cause over that period of time."

The IPA's Director of Marketing Janet Hull agrees. "There have been signs that attitudes have begun to move in favour of creative awards in recent years," she says. But the scepticism that had so troubled Donald Gunn in the 1990s still exists. "By no means do all advertisers believe that creative awards hold any commercial value. Creative awards are still often seen as a distraction from the business of selling."

"And it's difficult to pin down the reasons why," continues Peter. "I think it's a number of things. It's partly the excesses of the past… the clients who were around in the 1980s and 1990s probably did see a less business-like approach to creativity in agencies.

"I think another reason is the kind of stuff that gets taught in marketing, even today. Anyone who's gone into marketing has come out of it with classical marketing training, the kind of stuff that gets taught in colleges. It's so well off the pace, it's so out of touch with modern thinking and understanding of how the brain works. And if you've come from that kind of educational background you could be forgiven for thinking that how to sell a product is, you know, functional benefits, communication of messages; it's about hard selling. And all that creativity bit is loose-cannon thinking that occasionally works out but, by and large, is pretty dangerous stuff.

"And then of course there's the cosh that's on marketing these days. Marketing used to be a much more trusted discipline within companies. But if you talk to most CEOs these days they regard marketing as a pretty flaky discipline. It's not commercially focused and can't really be trusted. That's true of Chief Executives and certainly true of Finance Directors who see marketing as flaky and loose. And if they think marketing is flaky you can bet your bottom dollar they think ad agencies are flaky squared. You know, off in la la land."

Peter's ongoing study, 'The Link Between Creativity and Effectiveness',[27] has sought to answer the same question that Donald asked years earlier. Only, to put a more sturdy case to the CEOs and Finance Directors, he's asked the question with significantly more data, more independence[a] and more rigour.

"When I first spoke to Donald I said, 'I can't guarantee you're going to get positive findings, but the omens are pretty good'."

In 2007, along with DDB's Les Binet, Peter had published *Marketing in the Era of Accountability*, another combing of the IPA's databank for effectiveness clues.

"In it there's a whole section on communication strategy," explains Peter, "and what we found was that emotional campaigns are much more effective. And in particular, those campaigns that get talked about a lot – the ones we call 'fame' campaigns – they're the most effective of all. They're conspicuously the most effective campaigns out there.

---

a   How independent is Peter Field? "I don't work for the IPA" he says. "I'm an independent consultant – a subcontractor to them on a number of projects that involve data analysis. They use me when they want an independent analytical approach. I'm also not part of the agency world. I haven't been for the last 13 years. I do very little work directly with agencies. Almost all of my work is on the client side and I've no axe to grind. I'm not interested particularly in proving this link for the sake of it. And I certainly don't get any remuneration as a result of these findings. I just saw this as an interesting piece of analysis in the databank that I wanted to further. And the results are as they are, the data's there. Anyone can inspect that data, it's robust and in the public domain."

"I was fairly certain that creative judges would be heavily skewed toward, firstly, emotional campaigns, and secondly, ones that had this kind of talkability about them. I imagined that would be very much the kind of thing that creative judges would be looking for. So I felt there was a pretty good chance that creatively-awarded campaigns would be fishing in a pool of rich effectiveness because the creative judges would be looking for the right sort of things.

"That was the hypothesis, and that's how it turned out – that's exactly what they seem to be looking for. If you look at creatively-awarded campaigns they're much more likely to be emotional, and very much more likely to have generated these strong word-of-mouth effects and both of those things correlate with effectiveness.

"But even so, the extent to which they turned out to be more effective than non-creatively-awarded campaigns still remains astonishing to me – I still find it difficult to quite believe the extent of that difference."

The Link Between Creativity and Effectiveness, first published in 2010 and updated several times since, begins with 479 IPA case studies. These represent every campaign to have been recognised as effective at the IPA's Effectiveness Awards (globally considered the toughest and most credible advertising effectiveness awards programme) since 2000. Why 2000? This was the inaugural year of the Gunn Report, and so these 479 campaigns are those capable of being analysed according to *both* creative award and effectiveness performance.

Of these campaigns, 92 were creatively-awarded, and 387 were not, establishing the two groups to compare and contrast. At first glance, this seems to suggest that effective campaigns are predominantly *uncreative*, making more of a case for *uncreativity*. However, a deeper analysis reveals the opposite. "If you take the total number of ads made each year, about one in 7,000 pick up a creative award," says Peter, illustrating how rare creatively-awarded work is, and therefore how statistically unlikely it is to show up at effectiveness award shows. About a hundredth of a per cent of advertising in general is creatively-awarded. But among highly effective campaigns, i.e., campaigns effective enough to win an IPA Effectiveness Award, 24 per cent are creatively-awarded. That's an over-index of 168,000 for the statisticians out there, suggesting that creatively-awarded campaigns are orders of magnitude more likely to be effective.

"But this is not certain proof," the study hastens to remind us, "and so we shall examine whether the 24 per cent of creatively-awarded campaigns out-performed the 76 per cent of non-awarded campaigns in hard business terms."

Had the creatively-awarded group differed from the non-awarded group in any meaningful way it would have skewed the result. For example, say the creatively-awarded campaigns were all from growing categories, but the non-awarded ones were in stagnant categories, then the awarded campaigns would have had a head start. Peter was careful to contrast the two groups on measures of market share, category life stage, leader vs challenger, launches and re-launches, use of communication channel, and industry sector. He found that the

The 11:1 Efficiency Advantage of Creatively-Awarded Campaigns over Non-Creatively Awarded Campaigns

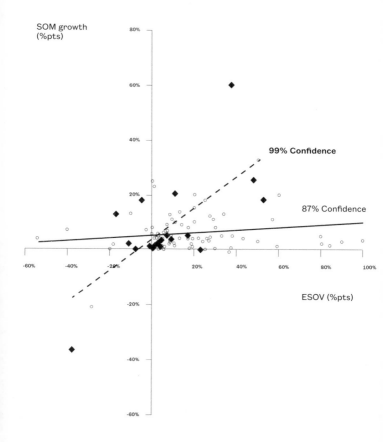

○ **Non-creatively awarded** ◆ **Creatively awarded**

SOM growth (%pts)

99% Confidence

87% Confidence

ESOV (%pts)

— **Non-Creatively Awarded Campaigns**
Average Share Growth:
0.5 points per 10 points of ESOV

····· **Creatively Awarded Campaigns**
Average Share Growth:
5.7 points per 10 points of ESOV

two groups were evenly matched across all measures. Safe in the knowledge that the fight was fair, Peter put the two cohorts into the ring.

His first enquiry was into the efficiency of each group. In *Marketing in the Era of Accountability,* he and Les Binet had coined the term 'excess share of voice' (ESOV), which describes the situation of a brand's share of advertising spend in its category being greater than its market share. The effect of ESOV was invariably that the brand's market share grew.

On average, if you bought ten points of ESOV, you would get 1.1 per cent market share growth. Very efficient campaigns would achieve more than 1.1 per cent share growth for ten points of ESOV, and less efficient ones would achieve less than 1.1 per cent.

He first calculated the ESOV effects of the non-awarded campaigns. They worked out at 0.5 per cent market share growth per ten points of ESOV. Well under the average. Next he measured the creatively-awarded campaigns. On average, they generated 5.7 per cent market share growth per ten points of ESOV. *Over 11 times greater than the non-awarded average.*

What this means is that the return on media investment for a highly creative campaign is on average 11 times higher. Or looking at it another way, to get the same result, you need to spend 11 times more media money on an uncreative campaign than you do on a highly creative one.

The intriguing second finding was that the creatively-awarded campaigns were much more *certain* to achieve that effectiveness result.

In the case of the non-awarded campaigns, the average was 0.5 per cent market share growth per ten points of ESOV. But this average was frequently deviated from, revealing a degree of confidence of 87 per cent.

In the case of the creatively-awarded campaigns, that degree of confidence was 99.9 per cent.

What this implies is that less creative campaigns are not only less efficient, but also less predictable than creatively-awarded ones – something of a departure from the perceived notion that a more creative approach is a less certain one.

"The paradoxical finding is that the correlation between creativity and efficiency of spend is stronger with creatively-awarded campaigns than with non-creatively-awarded ones," says Peter. "So the suggestion is in fact that creatively-awarded campaigns are more reliably effective than non-creatively-awarded ones. That flies in the face of accepted wisdom that creativity is a bit hit-and-miss. Clients in general management roles often have a preference for things that are less efficient but more certain rather than more efficient and less certain. There's that perception that creativity is very hit-and-miss. Although this paradoxical finding suggests that maybe that isn't true."

An old colleague of mine had a habit of dividing marketers into two groups – those he said were 'in it to win' and those who were 'in it not to lose'. What he meant is that some clients go for higher risk and higher reward in order to win big, and others go for lower risk and lower reward in order to minimise their risk of losing.

What Peter's work suggests is that whether you are in it to win, or in it not to lose, you're better off with a more creative approach. Creatively-awarded campaigns are shown to be both lower risk *and* higher reward.

Peter's next question was whether, beyond media spend efficiency, the creatively-awarded campaigns were better at generating what he calls 'large business effects'. Those are top-box scores for serious sales metrics such as penetration, share growth or profit growth (the kinds of results the finance director cares about, as opposed to softer communication tracking or brand health measures).

The analysis showed that at high levels of spend, the creatively-awarded campaigns were 10 per cent more likely to generate those 'large business effects' than the non-awarded ones.

More interestingly, at lower levels of spend the creatively-awarded campaigns performed even better. At 27 per cent more likely to generate 'large business effects', the creatively-awarded campaigns again showed much higher return on investment.

What followed was a hypothesis. "In theory," Peter thought, "if creativity is good for effectiveness then greater creativity ought to be better." So he asked whether those campaigns that are the *most* creatively-awarded are also the *most* effective.

Again it was Donald Gunn's work that enabled such a question to be asked. Each awarded campaign has a Gunn report score, which increases according to the quantity and quality of creative awards won.

"To pick up a point in the Gunn report," says Peter, "you have to have won a fairly important creative award. Not always quite as posh as Cannes, but these are the major creative awards. They refuse to reveal exactly which award schemes they count, because they don't want to be seen to prejudice award schemes. But we know that the famous ones are in there, the ones that most creative people respect around the world."

Peter was able to look at the creatively-awarded campaigns that had been the most effective, and see whether they also had the highest Gunn Report scores.

He divided the campaigns into three groups. The campaigns that hadn't won any creative awards, the campaigns that had scored between 1 and 3 points in the Gunn Report, and the campaigns that had scored 4 or more Gunn Report points.

The findings were conclusive. Compared with the non-creatively-awarded campaigns, the campaigns that had scored 1–3 Gunn Report points were almost 10 times as efficient. Better yet, the campaigns that had scored 4 or more Gunn Report points were over 16 times as efficient.

Last, Peter asked perhaps the most fascinating question of all – is creativity getting more effective?

To find the answer, he split the database in two. The campaigns from before 2004, and the campaigns from 2004 and later.

"Comparison of the efficiency of pre-2004 non-awarded campaigns with 2004 and post reveals a *marked* reduction in their efficiency." In fact their efficiency had halved. Which stood in stark contrast to

Creatively-Awarded Campaigns More Effective at Generating Large Business Effects at Both Low and High Spends

□ Non-creatively awarded   ■ Creatively awarded

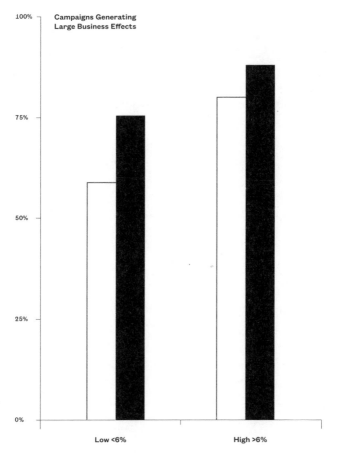

Excess Share of Voice

the creatively-awarded campaigns. "The efficiency of awarded campaigns appears to have *risen* markedly. The ratio of efficiency of creatively-awarded to non-awarded campaigns has in fact *grown* from around 3:1 to around 12:1."

The reason for this, Peter surmises, is to do with the growing role of social media.

"The association of creativity with fame may illuminate the earlier finding that awarded campaigns appear to be getting more efficient over time whereas non-awarded ones are getting less so. As the multi-channel world develops it creates new opportunities for brands to engage with consumers. Central amongst these is the ability to get consumers to share campaigns amongst their social networks. But as marketers are learning, the entry stakes for this are rising all the time: campaigns that do not surprise or inspire are unlikely to get shared. Creativity clearly feeds the motivation to share. By the same token the multi-channel world is progressively shutting out those brands that are unable to find the skills to compete on this new playing field."

To Peter, the data was conclusive. "The greater the level of creativity, the greater the level of effectiveness."

Or, as McKinsey & Company put it, "the more creative a campaign, the higher the likelihood that the featured product will sell."[28]

McKinsey had been told by the German marketing head mentioned in Chapter 1 that "creativity is irrelevant at best. Often, it is downright harmful to advertising success." So their Düsseldorf office spent 2006 finding out whether or not he was right.

The Most Creatively-Awarded Campaigns are Also the Most Effective

□ **1-2 Large Business Effects** ■ **2+ Large Business Effects**

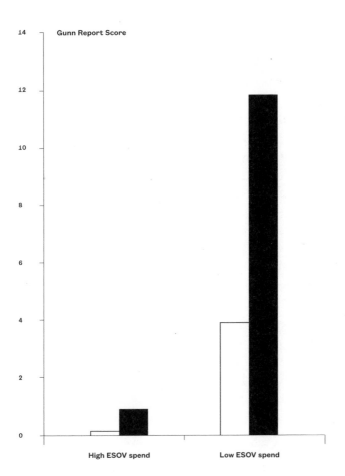

Some 100 television commercials submitted for the 2005 German effectiveness awards were examined, with changes in market share used as the measure of business impact.

They found that while the performance of less creative campaigns varied, the more creative campaigns were all high achievers in terms of business success.

They revealed what Donald Gunn had found a decade earlier and what Peter Field would find four years later: that more creative campaigns are indeed more effective, and more reliably effective.

They generate more 'large business results' than less creative campaigns. They're more efficient – they produce better results on much lower levels of media spend than less creative campaigns. And what's more, highly creative campaigns are more *certain* to produce those results than less creative campaigns.

The world's most prestigious management consulting firm[29] had clear advice for marketers. "Other things being equal," they said, "creativity is an advertiser's best bet."

In the years that followed, Peter continued to mine the IPA's growing databank for insights into creativity's effects. His research maintained that creatively awarded campaigns outperformed non-awarded ones on every metric. They were more likely to increase awareness, improve brand image, increase brand trust, drive penetration and increase market share. And they were twice as likely to be shared and talked about, drive differentiation, increase loyalty and lead to significant profit gains.

Until finally he hit upon one lone metric that the less creative campaigns won on: very short term sales gains. While 33 per cent of the non-awarded campaigns reported immediate sales gains, only 24 per cent of the creatively-awarded campaigns did.

As it turns out, if all you want to achieve is an immediate sales lift after running a campaign, "it remains true that you better just do something pretty dull and clunky. Hammer the message out, make it very dull and propositional."

But this advice comes with two health warnings. Firstly, in the fullness of time the creative campaigns outperform the uncreative ones on sales gains. Once campaigns have been in market more than six months, the total sales gains are larger for the creative campaigns. What sales advantage you might collect in the short term will be lost in the medium term.

Secondly, while rational and uncreative campaigns might outperform the creative campaigns on short-term sales, they under-perform on every single other measure on the marketing dashboard: awareness, brand image, brand trust, differentiation, penetration, loyalty, market share and profit gains.

In pursuing immediate sales effects we sacrifice medium term sales and *every other* brand and business metric. Buying a short-term sales gain is a costly business.

But what Peter's research has most recently revealed is that it doesn't have to be. "People have become better at exploiting their creative property and using it for short-term effect," says Peter, pointing to a trend in our aptitude for short-term creative effectiveness.

He found that certain highly creative campaigns managed to match the less creative ones even on short-term sales gains.

Those campaigns "are what I call multi-channel creativity – creative campaigns that pick up creative awards across multiple channels. They replicated that creativity across multiple channels and extended the creative boost to short-term sales activation. These are the ones that are really punching hard at the moment, cause they look at the same long-term benefits, but they capture the same sense of short-term urgency and really close that gap."

Peter uses examples such as John Lewis's 'The Bear and the Hare' campaign, winner of a gold Creative Effectiveness Lion in 2015, and Snickers' 'You're Not You When You're Hungry', the only campaign in the world to have won two Creative Effectiveness Lions as well as golds at both the UK's IPA Effectiveness Awards and the US Effies.

In both cases, those campaigns had core creative TV assets. But rather than copying and pasting onto traditional retail activations, they were highly creative about pushing the campaign idea into a wide range of channels, surrounding the consumer.

John Lewis' story of 'The Bear and the Hare' was turned into a bestselling kids book and an interactive e-book narrated by radio DJ Lauren Laverne that went to #2 in the UK app store. The song recorded for the television commercial by Lilly Allen stayed at #1 on the UK charts for three weeks. The characters of the ads were staged as social media personalities that thousands

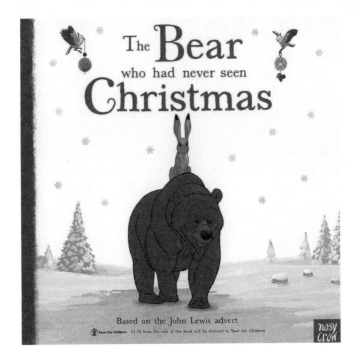

The children's book born of John Lewis' *The Bear and the Hare* campaign followed, and turned into merchandise that sold out in two weeks, going on to sell for three times the price on eBay.

The result was an immediate sales uplift to the tune of £142 million, leading to a Christmas profit of nearly £46 million, from a spend of under £6 million. John Lewis experienced its highest ever Christmas sales, and highest ever share of Christmas sales.

Snicker's global observation that we're not ourselves when we're hungry played out in local television commercials in many different markets and languages – but also in myriad paid and earned executions: internet memes appeared urging Obama to eat a Snickers; a German football club temporarily changed their logo to feature a ballerina rather than a footballer; Puerto Rican breakfast show DJs who played out-of-character music all morning; and some UK celebrities tweeted atypical messages, finally revealing it was all because they were hungry.

After three months in market in the US, Snickers reversed declining volume sales, growing at more than twice the category. Then as the work rolled out to other markets, global sales increased more than 15 per cent, tripling the category's performance.

"I don't think its good enough these days to say 'well look, you'll just have to bide your time, it'll come good in the end'," says Peter. "You have to find a way of making it work."

What Peter's studies are beginning to reveal is how advertisers can have their cake and eat it – by choosing one big core creative idea, then surrounding it not with prosaic retail executions, but with equally creative tactical ideas. The power of this symbiosis is that the value of the creative idea is activated sooner, yielding high short term gains, and then following through with all of the longer term advantages that we've come to expect from highly creative work.

"So these are the ones I'm trying to make the heroes of the story now," finishes Peter, "because they're the ones that show us the future."

Bill Bernbach

How creativity works

"I warn you against believing that advertising is a science."
— *Bill Bernbach, Doyle, Dane & Bernbach*

By the time DDB founder Bill Bernbach died in New York City in 1982, he'd made a case for creativity so strong it had completely redefined both the structure of advertising agencies and the nature of their product. During advertising's 'creative revolution', Bernbach put forward ideas about creativity that were expressed so persuasively and so memorably that they stuck just as fast as truths to the ideology of our industry.

But they weren't, in those days, known to be truths. Bernbach believed in creativity wholeheartedly, and expressed those beliefs with indomitable conviction. Albeit, they were only beliefs. Like everybody else, Bernbach had been exposed only to his own tiny set of personal experience.

Until a full decade after he died, there was no evidence that his words were any more than just great ads for creativity. There had been no academic interest in advertising creativity. Whether it worked or how it worked – these weren't questions being asked by researchers on anything other than a case-by-case basis in pre-testing or tracking research.

Half a century on, we know for sure that Bernbach was right. His words really were those of somebody with an innate understanding of human nature and its relationship with creativity.

Not only do we now know that creativity works, we also have a fairly deep understanding of how it makes advertising more effective, thanks to the work of several teams of university academics from across the world.

"I warn you against believing that advertising is a science," Bernbach said. And the creation of it can never be, for so many conspicuous reasons. But perhaps he would forgive us for borrowing from science to understand why he was right, and to revisit the unforgettable aphorisms he used to illuminate some of advertising's brightest years.

"If your advertising goes unnoticed,
everything else is academic."

Bernbach's inference was that more creative advertising is more likely to stand out and be noticed.

In 2002 researchers at Tilburg University in the Netherlands sought to explore the relationship between originality in advertising and the attention paid to that advertising.[30] Using eye-tracking technology, they observed the attention levels of consumers as they read two magazines containing 58 print advertisements ranging from unoriginal to highly original. Using infrared corneal reflection eye tracking, the participants' eye movements were recorded as they read the magazines. The originality of the ads was measured according to how surprising and unique the executions were, and how little they looked like other ads.

They found that increased levels of originality promoted increased and more intense attention to the advertisement and to the brand in those advertisements.

No fewer than four other groups of academics asked the same question about creativity and salience. They all reached the same conclusion.[31]

Creativity's first effect is that it makes advertising more likely to stand out and be noticed among the 3,000 or so commercial messages that consumers are besieged with daily.

"The difference between the forgettable and the enduring is artistry."

Bernbach believed that uncreative advertising would be forgotten, whereas more creative work would live on in the minds of consumers.

In 2005 research participants at the University of South Carolina were shown a TV show with ten minutes of advertising content embedded in the breaks. The study contrasted 40 Communication Arts award-winning commercials against a control group of 40 randomly selected 30-second spots from the same period that had not won any creative awards.[32]

Unaided recall was tested immediately after the show, and then again one week later.

The result in both cases was that the creative commercials were significantly (from two to nine times) more likely to be recalled unprompted than the control commercials.

Creativity's second effect is that it makes advertising more likely to be remembered, and more likely not to end up being one of the 2,998 messages that go unrecalled each day.

"Word of mouth is the best medium of all."

Bernbach said this decades ago. Although it might seem like common knowledge today, Bernbach realised the power of conversation long before it became fashionable. As described in the previous chapter, highly creative campaigns are far more likely to drive word of mouth, and campaigns that drive word of mouth have been shown to be the most effective of all from a hard business results point of view. Creativity's third effect is driving the brand out of paid-for media and into the conversations of consumers.

"Getting a product known isn't the answer. Getting it WANTED is the answer. Some of the best-known product names have failed."

Bernbach knew that spending vast amounts on uncreative advertising would buy brand awareness, but that brand awareness isn't in itself persuasive. He believed that a more creative approach would help persuade consumers to buy a product.

Creativity's fourth and most powerful effect is in making advertising more persuasive. Bernbach had ideas about why, exactly, people felt more persuaded by creative advertising. "You can say the right thing about a product and nobody will listen," he said. "You've got to say it in a way that people will feel in their gut. Because if they don't feel it, nothing will happen."

Bernbach believed in the ability of creativity to 'persuade' – on the basis that it made people more likely to listen and to believe the rational information contained within. Through connecting with people in a less rational and more visceral way, creativity breaks down the barriers of mistrust and scepticism, leaving consumers more likely to believe what the brand has to say.

In 2009 Professors at the University of Wisconsin-Milwaukee and Indiana University created a pool of 50 creative award-winning ads and 50 'average' TV ads randomly recorded from major TV networks. Subjects were shown a selection of the ads within a section of 'Entertainment Tonight', then questioned on the persuasiveness of those ads.[33]

The findings were that the creatively-awarded ads triggered greater purchase intent, and that this was because they measurably increased open-mindedness and curiosity. Consumers let their defences down more for the creative advertising, allowing themselves to be sold to more readily. "This is an important finding," said the researchers, "because consumers are often sceptical and closed-minded when processing information from a vested-interest source, so they are unlikely to change existing beliefs and attitudes based on ad claims. Accordingly, any strategy that can reduce resistance to persuasion and make consumers more open-minded can have a significant impact on brand purchase intentions."

> *"Properly practised creativity can make one ad do the work of ten."*

Bernbach was actually off a little on this one. Properly practised creativity can, as detailed in the previous chapter, make one ad do the work of 11.

And it does so not with some one-dimensional impact, but with a four-stage combination of effects that work together to deliver a result far more efficiently than advertising ever can without the power of creativity.

First, more creative advertising stands out from the clutter, differentiating itself among a daily barrage of 3,000 commercial messages. Then, it makes you remember it. It sticks in your mind to guide you toward the brand it is advertising in the days following its viewing. Thirdly, you're much more likely to talk about it with others, and those conversations have been shown to have the greatest effect of all on sales. And lastly, creativity persuades you. It breaks down your barriers of scepticism and cuts through your cognitive immune system, making you far more likely to believe the advertiser and to act on that belief.

That, according to two decades of academic research, is how creativity makes advertising more effective.

Product recall.

Volkswagen Golf Type I, 1974 model

It has been shown that, due to vibration, the **closing mechanism of the glove compartment** can be subject to wear. In the long run, in some cases, this might result in a more difficult handling of this mechanism. Even though no complaints have been registered, Volkswagen is making Golf Type I owners aware of this, as a precaution.

As this is not in line with the high standards of quality that Volkswagen has for its products, owners of the above-mentioned model are requested to go to www.volkswagen.nl/recall before 12 January 2008.

If necessary, Volkswagen will have the closing mechanism **replaced free of charge**. Volkswagen regrets any inconvenience caused. This is why Volkswagen offers dissatisfied customers **free servicing** for their car as compensation.

Volkswagen emphasizes that this only applies to the Volkswagen Golf Type I, 1974 model.

Once again, Volkswagen offers its apologies for any inconvenience caused.

Pon's Automobielhandel B.V. (Volkswagen importer)

Volkswagen's *Product Recall* — one of the brand's
15 creatively awarded campaigns of 2008.

The case for creative companies

"We'd been through the dark ages. And then we had the enlightenment."
— *Jim Stengel, former Global Marketing Officer, P&G*

At the 2009 Cannes International Festival of Creativity, the Advertiser of the Year award was presented to Volkswagen. Perennial darlings of the Côte d'Azur, the pre-emissions-scandal Volkswagen tallied over 150 Cannes Lions including five Grands Prix and the award for the best commercial ever for Bill Bernbach's 1963 Beetle *Snow plow* spot.

The Advertiser of the year award recognised a particularly fertile 2008 for Volkswagen and their agencies DDB and Almap BBDO. No less than 15 separate campaigns for the brand were awarded at Cannes, D&AD and Clio. In terms of advertising creativity, it was a truly exceptional year, even for a brand like Volkswagen.

But that wasn't the only remarkable thing about Volkswagen's 2008. In a record year of trading for the car-maker, Volkswagen's share price swelled 89 per cent to an all-time high of €283.[34]

The previous year, when many of those award-winning campaigns ran, the stock market performance was similarly impressive at 74 per cent growth.

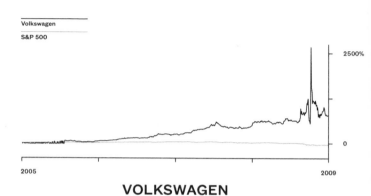

VOLKSWAGEN

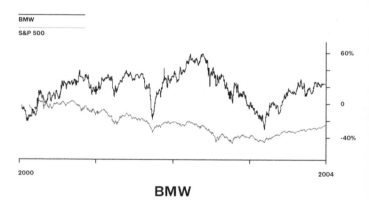

BMW

Across the 2000s, Volkswagen's average annual share price rise was an admirable 46 per cent. But during the period of their most abundant creativity, the gain was almost double at 82 per cent. During that same period the S&P 500 fell nearly 16 per cent,[35] illustrating how brightly Volkswagen outshone the market.

It would be far-fetched to claim that those award-winning campaigns drove the VOW.DE share price, but it's interesting to observe that Volkswagen's most prolific period of stock-market success coincides precisely with their most prolific period in terms of creativity. We'd be forgiven for passing it off as a happy coincidence, but what's intriguing is how eerily often this coincidence seems to occur.

"For 20 years I'd been going to Cannes," says Airbnb Chief Marketing Officer Jonathan Mildenhall, "and I'd observed this correlation between financial performance and marketing success." Jonathan was previously Coca Cola's VP of Global Advertising Strategy and Content Excellence, and in fact inspired this chapter of the book when he told a friend of mine he had noticed consistent examples of Advertiser of the Year companies showing record stock-market performance. Admittedly, at the time I was a little sceptical of advertising's ability to impact stock prices. So I had a look for myself.

Cannes began the twenty-first century by naming Sony its 2000 Advertiser of the Year. The award was presented to Sony CEO Nobuyuki Idei, primarily for TBWA's work on PlayStation.

Sony's 1999 year was extraordinary. The share price increased a staggering 242 per cent, ten times the S&P 500. On 28 February 2000, Sony's stock hit an all-time high of $149.72, a figure it has not reached since.[36]

Anheuser Busch told the same story the next year. Just like the others, their 2001 Advertiser of the Year award was preceded by two years of share price rises that eclipsed the S&P 500.[37]

The 2002 Advertiser of the Year was Swatch. During the 1999–2001 period, the S&P 500 didn't grow a cent. Swatch, however, doubled their share value with one of the steepest periods of stock market growth on record.[38]

The ever-bullish Nike, 2003's Advertiser of the Year, came out of the events of 9/11 in far better shape than most. "We decided to cross the threshold of September 11," wrote CEO and founder Phil Knight in his 2002 annual report. "Eight months later we delivered a 14 per cent increase in earnings, and beat the S&P by 45 points... a defining moment... a Nike moment."[39]

In 2004 BMW received the Advertiser of the Year award for, among others, Fallon's 'BMW Films' campaign. Following a 12 per cent sales increase after the first series of the films,[40] BMW's share price grew 16 per cent in 2003, a huge rally during a highly turbulent period for the stock market.[41]

The next year, PlayStation won Advertiser of the Year. As a sub-brand of Sony, PlayStation doesn't exist as an independent financial entity and thus there's no stock market performance to report. However, the years leading up to 2005 were instrumental in the PS2 becoming the world's bestselling gaming console, having shifted in excess of 100 million units.[42]

In 2006, Adidas was announced as Cannes Lions Advertiser of the year at the end of a period of 35 per cent share price growth, more than four times the S&P 500.[43] Again this was a record result for the company, following a wave of exceptional creative work. US sales lifted by 11 per cent,[44] and the company experienced its most vigorous stock market performance in history.

At the end of 2006, six months before Cannes crowned Honda their 2007 Advertiser of the year, the Japanese car-maker hit their highest recorded share price of $38.50,[45] growing 24 per cent against a an S&P 500 index of 10.35 per cent. A series of extraordinary campaigns in 2005 and 2006, including 'Cog' and 'Grrr', had driven a turnaround in perceptions of the Honda brand and a 28 per cent increase in UK sales.[46]

In 2008, Cannes' Advertiser of the year was P&G. The story of marketing chief Jim Stengel's creative ambition for P&G is legendary, culminating in 14 Cannes Lions in 2007 for an organisation historically pilloried for its conservatism and unoriginality.

On 12 December 2007, P&G hit their all-time share price high of $74.67.[47] Two months earlier, in an article titled 'P&G Share Price Soars', Cosmetics International magazine reported that "declining consumer spending, a jittery US housing market and rising interest rates might worry some companies, but not Procter & Gamble. The share price of the personal care giant has hit almost $70, up 20 per cent from under $62 a share back in July."[48]

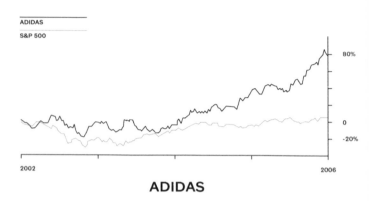

ADIDAS

UNILEVER

Hot on Volkswagen's heels was Unilever, whose 2010 award followed the ravages of the global financial crisis. But as the S&P 500 sank like a stone with a 25 per cent loss in 2008/2009, Unilever kept its head above water, posting a 5 per cent gain.[49]

Ikea and Mars, 2011 and 2012's recipients, are privately owned companies, but despite the lack of share price as a measure, their commercial indicators were strong. Forbes reported that Mars global sales grew 7.1 per cent on revenues of $30 billion.[50] And in their 2010 Yearly Summary, Ikea's CEO Mikael Ohlsson said "the IKEA Fiscal Year 2010 has been very exciting. We have moved forward in line with our vision of creating a better life for the many people and our sales grew by 7.7 per cent."[51]

In 2013, Cannes Lions renamed their Advertiser of the Year award 'Creative Marketer of the Year'. But the idea remained the same – an honorary award given to companies who have made a public declaration that they are putting creativity at the heart of what they do, who've won more Lions year on year for a number of years, and who have won across categories, and geographies, with different agency partners.

That year, Coca Cola won the prize. Coke had excelled on all measures. With the appointment of a Chief Creative Officer back in 2005, along with Jonathan Mildenhall being hired specifically to raise the creativity of Coke's global advertising output in 2007, the company were well known for their investment in creativity. And they'd been a juggernaut at Cannes. Their 'Open Happiness' brand platform had inspired agencies all across the world to produce a torrent of Lion-winning campaigns, culminating in a staggering 32 Lions in 2013. From the launch of 'Open Happiness' in 2008 until the end of 2012, the S&P 500 only barely recovered the ground lost from the financial crisis. Coke's stock grew nearly 100 per cent.[52]

McDonald's, 2014's Creative Marketer of the Year, looks like the one that got away. Its well documented challenges saw it stagnate against the S&P 500 toward the end of 2013. But it is worth noting that in the four years up until October that year, they had decisively outpaced the stock market, growing their share price more than 50 per cent.[53]

In 2015, things returned to normal, with Creative Marketer of the Year Heineken growing their share price by more than 22 per cent in 2014, almost doubling the S&P 500. And that was a typical year. From 2009 until 2014, Heineken's stock grew 250 per cent. The S&P 500? 135 per cent.[54]

"The Procter & Gamble of 15 years ago basically said 'humour has no role in advertising'," remembers Jim Stengel. "Procter & Gamble 15 years ago said 'we'll never go to Cannes'."

Stengel speaks with measured conviction, but his tone still manages to convey how archaic he considered those bygone edicts to be. In 2001, after 18 years with P&G, Stengel was named Global Marketing Officer. His twin legacies are transforming P&G from an archetypal conservative FMCG marketer to a highly creative brand builder, and assisting in almost doubling P&G's revenue by the time he departed in 2008.

"Back in 2001, the company was in a funk," he says. "The results were not strong. People were not inspired. So when I got into the role I did a lot of talking to our agencies, a lot of talking to our people, I went outside the company and talked to different people, people I respected in all kinds of industries. I remember talking to Leo Burnett about Michael Conrad's work on creativity back in the 1990s.[55] I did some benchmarking myself, I commissioned a very special study to look into companies and brands that grew faster than P&G and what could I learn about them. I looked at what brands within P&G were growing faster. I did an awful lot of exploration early in my role, and I worked with my team to say 'okay, what do we want to be here? Are we okay with being an average consumer products company?' Because we had fallen. Our results had really stalled. So we kind of rallied around this idea of being the best. We wanted to be the best in the world. And I'm not sure P&G had ever been that bold. They always wanted to be the best in their category. But we said, you know, versus Apple, versus Nike, versus anyone, we want to be up there. The reputation, results, creativity and people. And we were nowhere close to being that. Not even close. P&G was very left brain, very dogmatic, and the company quite frankly didn't know what to do with the right side of the brain."

Those discussions and benchmarking studies led to P&G thinking very differently about creativity, even to the extent of flying their marketing team to the Cannes festival in 2003 for the first time in the company's history.

"We really raised our standards on creativity. And going to Cannes was a part of that. Going to Cannes was a strong message inside of the company, and outside, that things had changed. That expectations were different, and that we really did want to attract the best talent within our agencies, and have them be as proud of our work as any client in the world. So Cannes was certainly part of that strategy. But it wasn't the only part. I got the agencies together for a regular rhythm. I would get Kevin Roberts, Maurice Levy, the head of Leo Burnett which was Linda Wolf at the time, we would get Ed Meyer at Grey, all the heads of our major agencies, and I'd put them in one room for two days. I'd get in front of them and say 'here's what I'm trying to do'. And I'd bring in our CEO and say, 'A.G., just tell them honestly how you're seeing the business, the brands, the people'. And by the way I had the creative heads of each agency. We had Droga in there, we had Isherwood, we had Conrad, we had Mellors, and we put them all in a room and I said 'here's what we're trying to do', and actually we approached it like a team. And out of one of those meetings came the idea to go to Cannes. I brought in a couple of new agencies, because I thought we could learn a lot from them. I brought in Wieden+Kennedy. I brought in TBWA\-Chiat\Day. With Gillette we got BBDO. We went to Cannes. We instituted awards. We really changed our standards. We celebrated great creativity in lots of different ways."

Around the same time as Jim Stengel was setting P&G's new creative agenda, BMW and their agency Fallon were enjoying the runaway success of their 'BMW Films' campaign. That work had been the product of a period of soul-searching not unlike P&G's.

"In 1999," says ex-BMW CMO Jim McDowell, "we decided that we wanted to do a major branding effort for BMW. The problem was, every time we saw the work we just weren't satisfied with it. It just didn't seem as though it was making enough of a big brand statement for BMW. Our agency had been making proposals to us for more than a year. Then we said, maybe we're too structured in terms of the way that we approach our brand understanding. We had lots of rules about how you'd project the BMW brand."

Jim took the decision to challenge some of the conventional wisdom around brand management to try to open up the creative thinking.

"We had very specific perspectives on how BMW needed to be pictured in any kind of television advertising, how they needed to be photographed, what kind of language, tonality we wanted, and we thought maybe the problem with this branding effort is that we just have too many rules."

So they went to Fallon with a new brief. "Give us some ideas where you break one or another of the rules that we've set, so we can see if maybe it's our rules that are hemming you in. So then they came back and said, 'We have an idea, but it's not for television.' And we said okay, so print? And they said 'No, it's not print either.' The idea is to do a series of amazing short films on the internet, and that they'd probably be the most exciting thing that most people had ever seen on their computer screen."

P&G and BMW's stories aren't uncommon. In my research of Advertiser of the Year and Creative Marketer of the Year companies, the most common theme was marketing chiefs who had changed the culture and the system to allow for better work.

"Most companies will say 'we like creativity, and we want to do creativity'," says Søren Hagh, Heineken's Executive Director of Global Marketing. "But Heineken actually *does* creativity. It takes creativity extremely seriously."

In the years leading up to their Creative Marketer of the Year award, Heineken had instigated major changes in their business to ensure they didn't just pay lip service to creativity. "Heineken was hugely committed to the idea that creativity makes a massive difference," says Hagh, "but while we were very committed to creativity we lacked a framework for delivering great creativity. So we were talking a lot about it, we were really trying, but the framework wasn't there. We asked ourselves whether we could increase our batting average. You're always going to get some right and some wrong, can we improve our chances of getting things right?"

Taking inspiration from Leo Burnett's '7plus' creativity scale, Heineken developed their own way of measuring their creative work objectively, everywhere in the world.

"We created this common language of creativity. We realised that we talked a lot about this stuff but we didn't speak the same language. What is great creativity? That was not clearly defined. So we set out to establish that. We created what we call the Creative Ladder. The Creative Ladder is a one-to-ten scale where one is destructive, directly negative for the business, you know, destroying the brand, right to ten, which is legendary, things that will live way beyond our lifetimes. Every piece of creative we work on can be judged on this scale."

The Creative Ladder created not only a common language, but also an easy way to categorise ideas and reject lower forms of creativity that all too often make their way through a traditional research and approval process.

"We very quickly realised that the really interesting place on the ladder is a four. A four is what we call 'cliché' – advertising that repeats the codes of the industry. And for all our hard work, we realised that much of what we do, and much of what our competitors do is basically telling our consumers what they already know about beer. Which is nice, and inoffensive, but also extremely dangerous, because its not breaking through, its not really doing anything for your brand, and it's the kind of stuff that might not get you fired, so it's safe, but it's also the sort of stuff that burns a lot of money. So Creativity at Heineken always needs to be beyond a four. Five is the absolute minimum, and five is what we call 'ownable' advertising. Ownable advertising is true to my brand, only I can deliver that, and in many ways that can actually be good enough to succeed. However, what we also believe is that we live more and more in a world where messages spread not by advertisers but by peers, and by social networks in different shapes and forms. And that's why we believe that the real creativity that's going to win long-term is what we call 'Breakthrough Creativity', which is seven or higher on the ladder. Breakthrough Creativity creates talkability. It's creativity that you, for one reason or another, are willing to share with your peers. Breakthrough Creativity is what we believe is going to define the future of great creativity. So that language is one thing we did."

It is the embedding of this language into the behaviour of the organisation that is most impressive. In Amsterdam, Heineken created their Global Commerce University – a school that all new hires go through to learn how to put into practice the company's brand building principles.

"With the creativity workstream, we decided to roll out this new approach not just with our internal people, but also with our partners. So we've taken literally thousands of our people through our master classes on creativity. It's about learning, but it's also about actually doing it, actually starting to work with this language on specific pieces of local creativity."

Heineken also made an astute observation about the sustainability of their creative ambition.

"The biggest fear that we have in our organisation is that when you're doing well, people start telling you that you're great – and the biggest risk is that you start believing that. You start leaning back and becoming complacent, becoming happy with your own work. And this is the one thing that we're trying very hard to avoid. So we have created what we call 'creative councils' – ongoing councils that we have around the world consisting of the best internal marketers from Heineken, but also our best partners – the best creative directors from our agencies and so on, the best strategy people we can find. These creative councils really judge our work. We take all the work we're producing, we put it in front of the creative council, and we typically spend a full day discussing the merits of different pieces of creativity – both of our own work and the best we find in the markets, not just in beer or drinks, but anywhere in the market. We ask 'how do we truly score against all of this work'.

"The idea with this is both to really embed the use of this language in the organisation, but also to hold us accountable to this journey and really make sure that we don't get self-satisfied, but actually we are truly good when we compare ourselves to the very best in the world. So those are some of the principles we've been working on. And we're seeing an enormous embrace of this journey in the organisation."

Convention so often stifles creativity – and what these marketing leaders all had was an acute sense of when to think beyond convention to ensure creativity flourished.

At Coca-Cola, Jonathan Mildenhall led a team that took a highly unconventional approach to developing and validating the 'Open Happiness' brand platform.

"We were working with Wieden+Kennedy on a global basis and then we worked with the local agencies

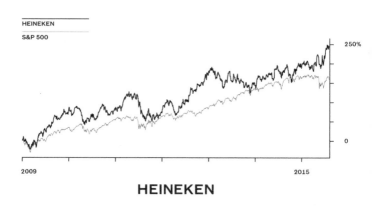

HEINEKEN

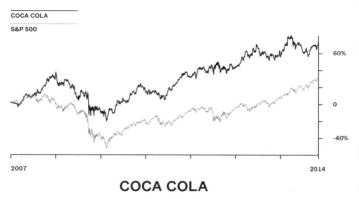

COCA COLA

(from Open Happiness to Cannes Creative Marketer of the Year)

in local markets to develop the proof of concept. The interesting thing was we proved out the concept not through research but through creative development in Latin America, Europe Asia and South Africa markets."

What Mildenhall understood was that the true test of a big, transformative, sustainable idea is not so much whether it'll research well, but whether it's capable of consistently inspiring highly creative executions from agencies all over the world. A good strategy on paper might produce an initial campaign that researches well. But few 'good' strategies are truly repeatable – and research can't identify them. The much surer way is to work with creative people to validate whether in fact the idea can be expressed powerfully in many different ways.

"The idea behind the 'Open Happiness' campaign positions Coke as 'the antidote to modern-day woes'. Modern-day woes can be things like isolation, so teen-agers not connecting with each other, things like fatigue, so people being tired at the end of the day and they need a little pick-me-up to get on with their homework, or it can be things like people being suspicious of each other and not actually communicating across borders. There are lots of modern-day woes that a little bit of Coca-Cola can help relieve. We needed to understand how this idea translated, what was the Latin American version of the antidote to modern-day woes? What's the European version of the antidote to modern-day woes? The Indian version? The Chinese version? It was a process that took us only three months, it was incredi-bly fast, and we basically proved out its global relevance through creative development as opposed to research."

That 'proving out' of a creative strategy by engaging agencies to 'test' how it would work in practise is an innovative approach – one which takes into account the realities of creativity, and one which led to one of the world's most powerful and effective brand platforms.

Later in his tenure, and upon completion of Coke's 'Content 2020' global communications strategy, Mildenhall rejected the convention of marketing communication strategies being rolled out globally by visiting each market and teaching marketing departments and agency partners individually – which is the traditional method for most multinationals.

"At the time we were working with 2,000 agencies from different genres – shopper-marketing, digital, social, advertising, mobile, content creation etc. I said to my boss Wendy Clark: 'We have a choice. I can spend the next five years traveling all our markets, meeting all the agencies individually, getting them to sign NDAs, doing workshop after workshop. But in truth I'll probably go around 5% of the agencies over the next 5 years and we'll miss this opportunity.'"

So he didn't. Instead, he created a film explaining the strategy,[56] which included a renewed commitment to creativity and frameworks for delivering it. And in an affront to corporate convention, he launched it publicly, meaning competitors often saw it before Coke's own people.

"The thing that surprised the entire industry, was that we put it out online, we made it public. I actually introduced it live at Cannes, to literally the entire industry – the creative industry, the media industry. And then we put it out online the day that I presented it to Cannes. I remember watching the faces of the audience as I narrated the film. On one side of the auditorium I saw my Coca-Cola family faces beaming with pride. On the other side of the auditorium I saw the PepsiCo posse recording the whole thing on their phones, faces getting redder and redder as each chapter unfolded. In fact, the first question that any of the journalists asked of Joe Tripodi (Coke's then Chief Marketing Officer) was: 'Are you crazy? Are you not concerned that Pepsi is going to take a look at this?' And Joe's response was simply superb: 'Pepsi may have our thinking, but they don't have our brands and they don't have our people, so they won't know what to do with the thinking'. It was so brave, it was so transparent, it made me truly proud to be working at such a confident and generous company – Coca-Cola at its best."

It was a hugely progressive way to approach the question of how to get his thinking out to the markets – and an ingenious way to use the creative community to hold their Coke clients to the strategy.

"Giving it to all of the agencies meant having all the agencies use it as a creative force against the more conservative parts of the Coca-Cola system. All of the agencies could point to this public thing. 'Hey Coca-Cola Marketing Director, we want you do great work, and look – this thing that's come from Coca-Cola Atlanta is out in the real world and it's getting an awful lot of traction!' So all of the agencies – because it was all in there, were all using that as the 'transcendent brief'. That was the North Star. Regardless of the tactical brief agencies had been given in the market. They had to answer the tactical requirements yes, but they had to also answer this North Star. That was the genius thing, because it really gave all of our ambitious creative partners the ammunition against the more conservative mind-set that naturally happens in multi-national organisations."

Creatively focused marketing leaders are clearly something of a precursor to winning Creative Marketer of the Year. But the common factor among those companies was not simply creatively focused marketers, but how those marketers were operating within organisations with a much broader creative agenda. Companies in the thick of periods of increased creativity in everything they did.

Erich Stamminger, Adidas President and CEO, was Head of Global Marketing up until 2006 when he became CEO. One of the architects of 'Impossible is Nothing', he used the creative spirit of that external brand positioning to drive culture and innovation throughout Adidas. "For each and every member of the Adidas family," he said, "'Impossible is Nothing', this attitude, this philosophy, has become part of our daily lives and our language."[57]

Innovating relentlessly through the early days of 'Impossible is Nothing', Adidas launched the Adidas-1 (the world's first intelligent shoe), opened their innovative Sports Performance Centre retail stores all over the world, launched Project Fusion, the world's first completely integrated training system, created the +F50 TUNIT – the first modular football boot and established design partnerships with Stella McCartney and Yohji Yamamoto. Extraordinary growth followed, and across the decade of 'Impossible is Nothing', Adidas grew from a €4.6 billion brand to one worth almost €8 billion.[58]

It's a similar story for BMW. "Without a doubt that was a really good period for BMW in the United States," says McDowell. "We had year after year of consecutive growth, and we still continued after September 11. That was a time when people were really unsettled in the United States, and BMW still had pretty robust sales."

That business success coincided with a wider agenda of innovation. "It was a very good period for innovation in the United States for BMW. In the late 1990s, BMW made a lot of changes to their cars to make them just perfect for the US market, and that was something we were benefiting from as we headed into the 2000s. And that effort at BMW led to the first Z3 launch. It was the first time BMW built a two-seat sports car for the mass market. The car was built in South Carolina, and it was introduced as James Bond traded in his Aston Martin for a BMW."

A decade later, Heineken's culture of innovation was similar. "It's a public company," says Søren Hagh, "but the Heineken family owns a controlling stake. And actually, that makes a very big difference. The family has a true dedication to creativity. And certainly when you talk to our CEO, or any of his direct reports, you will feel this massive dedication for delivering great creativity at all levels of what we do. I'm often amazed when I talk to our supply chain colleagues, with the kind of ingenuity they come up with in terms of delivering new product solutions, new ways of bringing things to market in innovative ways – its certainly not something I've seen in many other organisations."

In the case of Volkswagen, their business success accelerated as CEO Martin Winterkorn arrived fresh from completing Audi's design-led renaissance. He came with plans to innovate heavily and grow Volkswagen to replace Toyota as the world's largest car-maker.

At Honda, the 'Power of Dreams' campaign built on the imagination and creative passion of founder Soichiro Honda and engineer Kenichi Nagahiro, who completely recreated the diesel engine for Honda.

In the case of Swatch, Cannes Lions made specific mention of founder and CEO Nicolas Hayek's imaginative spirit. "This honour recognises the creative and innovative talents demonstrated by Mr Hayek, be it in Swatch product development or in Swatch advertising." Besides making the world's most creative watches, Hayek also created the Smart Car, in a joint venture with Mercedes-Benz, and served as member of a number of high-profile European government councils aimed at developing strategies for stimulating innovations for the future.

And of course, Coca-Cola's journey extended well outside of the marketing department too – in large part kick-started by the marketing campaign. "Coke was enjoying a creative renaissance across the business," says Mildenhall. "Everybody believed, powerfully, in the brand. Everybody from the truck driver and the bottlers and the buyers in different retail organisations – everybody just believed that Coke was back. It all happened around Open Happiness. Open Happiness gave the entire system the reason to believe in Coca-Cola again."

That renewed belief in Coca-Cola saw the company out of the doldrums and into a seven-year era of growth and success, even in the face of economic turmoil. "In 2007, the share price was at an all time low," says Mildenhall. "The shareholders were not happy about it, the senior leadership was not happy about it. A new Chief Exec was bought in to try and turn it around. And then of course the recession hit. But the recession hit at the same time that this new global co-creative idea hit. And what was beautiful was that Coca-Cola began to pull away from the drag of the global financial crisis. So while all other stocks started to plummet, Coca-Cola's stocks started to rise. Over the course of five years, the value of the company, the relevance of Coca-Cola, and the creativity of Coca-Cola was just building and building. The Open Happiness campaign has become Coke's most value-creating campaign in its history when you look at share price and the most in volume – there was more Coca-Cola drank the year we received Creative Marketer of the Year than in any previous year in our history. Share price had never been greater and volume sales had never been greater – there were more mouths touching Coca-Cola bottles than ever before."

"We'd been through the dark ages," says Stengel of P&G, "and then we had the enlightenment. A.G. Lafley [P&G's CEO at the time] was a wonderful leader and he pretty much said to all of us, 'I want all of us to create, to innovate, to think differently'. He said to the R&D head: 'We think we know better than everyone else. We think we have the best scientists, you know, 1,100 PhDs, we have 25,000 patents, blah blah blah.' He said, 'Well, you know, there are a lot of people outside this company who are really smart. What if half of our innovation could be sourced from outside the company? I'd like you to try that. And I'd like you to measure it.' So of course that totally disrupted how they worked. And all of a sudden we'd developed these internet-based platforms where we'd put problems out and have scientists in Russia and China and India solve them. And A.G. was famous for saying, 'We've gone from 1,100 R&D people to, like, 12 million, and didn't raise our overheads!'"

P&G didn't just become more creative in its advertising, it became more creative in everything it did.

"It was a period where we made design much more important, we named a head of design, we put design people on our R&D teams, we contracted with the world's best design firms, people like Ideo. We would do management meetings in design firms. In research we got more interesting, we stopped doing a lot of silly research where you look backwards, we did a lot more experiential research where we got ourselves involved. We would spend a week in a village studying a problem. Sometimes we'd put teams away for three months immersed in a brand restage. It was a period of great innovation across the company, and advertising was part of that."

"People were saying in the early 2000s, this company is as big as it's going to get, where else can they go?"

Stengel concludes with the results of P&G's creative agenda. "We doubled our size. We went from about $43 billion to about $83 billion in basically seven years. Our margins went up ten points. We went from nine billion-dollar brands to 25. And our earnings per share went up four-fold. So, you know, fantastic. Like double, you know, there was no question about the results."

The Cannes Creative Marketer of the Year award is all about creative advertising, "presented to advertisers who have distinguished themselves for inspiring innovative marketing of their products and who embrace and encourage the creative work produced by their agencies."

The companies who've been most tenacious in their pursuit of great advertising creativity have been among the ones outperforming the stock market and enjoying historic periods of financial prosperity.

And in every case, the leaders of those companies created a culture of innovation that advertising creativity was symptomatic of, but which extended well beyond advertising and into the culture, the product, the very day-to-day activities of those companies. A creative day-to-day that produced the most extraordinary results in the history of some of the world's most illustrious companies.

The case for fame

"Will someone look at this and want to share it?"

— *John Mescall, Global Executive Creative Director, McCann Worldgroup*

In 2011 I was lucky enough to be invited to judge the inaugural Cannes Creative Effectiveness Lions. It was the first time a leading awards show had undertaken to celebrate the work that was both highly creative *and* highly effective. I thought it was great. Why set our sights on being either 'creative' *or* 'effective', when we could be truly ambitious and demand both?

What I also loved about it was that as an industry we would build a collection of work to learn from. I've always enjoyed spending time showing clients great work. It always gets them thinking bigger, and often leads to them signing off better work themselves. The best campaigns of all to show them are the ones that are both highly creative *and* highly effective. Like everybody, clients get *inspired* by highly creative work. But they *learn* from highly effective work. Open up a conversation about work that's both highly creative *and* highly effective, and behaviour really starts to change.

What a great help it would be if we had a collection of campaigns that both agencies and clients could get inspired by and learn from together.

A year later, Donald Gunn asked if I would contribute something to the Gunn Report, and I remember thinking what a perfect platform that would be to grow our collection of creative and effective campaigns.

For many years, Donald had been collecting up campaigns from the Gunn Report that had shown measurable commercial effects. These 'Bullets From Gunn' mini-case studies can be accessed on the Gunn Report's website, and put some key effectiveness metrics around some of the world's best work. I wanted to help build on this great resource by bringing in the rigour of the Effie Awards judging process. We agreed to look at the campaigns that had won both a gold Cannes Lion for creativity and a gold Effie award for effectiveness – 'the glorious double' as Donald likes to say. We decided to call them 'Cases for Creativity'. Like the Creative Effectiveness Lion winners and Donald's 'Bullets', these would give us a group of campaigns that I hoped we could all be inspired by and learn from.[59]

To date, the collection includes 43 Creative Effectiveness Lions winners, 33 Cases for Creativity, and more than 200 Bullets from Gunn. Many of the campaigns appear in all three lists.

I have used these campaigns in workshops with client organisations all over the world. A key part of those workshops is having the clients look at the campaigns and spot the consistencies. To form a kind of checklist of attributes of truly creative and effective work. In my experience, clients often come to creative reviews with a checklist in their heads. And often the rules they had made worked at cross-purposes to effectiveness. I wanted clients to create a new set of rules. To base their checklists on what really defines highly effective creative work.

Clients invariably arrive at pretty similar lists. When you look at all of the world's most creative and effective work, there are some clear themes. And the clearest, by far, is that every single one of the examples has exploded on social media, being widely shared and generating what effectiveness researcher Peter Field calls 'fame' effects.

"Those campaigns that get talked about a lot," says Field, "the ones we call 'fame' campaigns – they're the most effective of all. They're conspicuously the most effective campaigns out there."

The power of a campaign such as Old Spice's 'The Man Your Man Could Smell Like' was in how it exploded online, earning an audience orders of magnitude larger than its media spend could ever have achieved. In its first week, the campaign was viewed more than 40 million times online, as Old Spice cemented a new place in global popular culture. Year on year sales grew 125 per cent during the six-month campaign – a feat which would have simply been impossible with advertising that merely communicated to a traditional media audience. For that result, Old Spice won the Grand North American Effie in 2011.

Look at any of the world's most creative and effective campaigns over the past decade and it is the same. Coca-Cola's 'Share a Coke', American Express's 'Small

Business Saturday', Dove's 'Real Beauty Sketches', Volvo's 'Live Test Series', Chipotle's 'Cultivate a Better World', Oreo's 'Daily Twist', Metro Melbourne's 'Dumb Ways to Die'. They're all examples of ideas that earned their right to be shared – and generated huge fame for their brands and causes.

"Fame campaigns work by getting the brand talked about and generally making it more famous," says Field. "This is not the same thing as advertising designed to raise brand awareness (which most advertising seeks to do) – it is about creating perceptions of being the brand that is 'making waves'. This encourages brand usage by creating perceptions that the brand is bigger and 'more important' than before."

This wasn't merely conjecture. The IPA's analysis of 880 marketing case histories showed that those campaigns that generated fame achieved an effectiveness success rate significantly higher than campaigns that were simply emotional in their content, persuasive in their argument or rational in their messaging. More than any other kind of campaign, 'fame' campaigns drove very large effects on hard business measures such as sales, market share or profit.

Three years later, the IPA report 'The Link Between Creativity and Effectiveness' found a distinct correlation between creatively-awarded campaigns and levels of 'fame'.

"The most significant difference between creatively -awarded and non-awarded campaigns was in the scale of the fame effects they generated; specifically online and offline buzz. Creatively-awarded campaigns were twice as likely to generate very large fame effects than non-awarded campaigns."

The study went on to make the astute observation that while you can buy awareness, you can't buy fame. That awareness (which correlates very loosely with effectiveness) is dependent on money, while fame (which correlates very tightly with effectiveness) is dependent on creativity.

Today, the link between creativity and effectiveness is simpler than it has ever been. Effectiveness is most efficiently driven by campaigns that create fame. Fame is most efficiently achieved with creativity.

So the first thing clients tend to put down on their checklists is: 'is this the kind of idea that people will share?'

The conversation then quickly turns to what sort of ideas tend to be shared.

The easiest theme to spot is the multi-channel nature of fame-driving campaigns. Outside of a scant handful of exceptions, people share ideas that aren't media-specific. Today it's pretty extraordinary for a TV commercial to go viral like Old Spice's did in 2010. The ideas that explode tend to be ones like 'Dumb Ways to Die', the most shared public service announcement in history.

'Dumb Ways to Die' was firstly a song. It was released and publicised like a song – with a music video on YouTube and a smattering of traditional and online media driving people to the video. They sold the song on iTunes and 77,000 people paid money for it. And they followed through with 'pledge' activations

Metro Melbourne's *Dumb Ways to Die*; American Express'
Small Business Saturday; Intermarché's *Inglorious Fruits & Vegetables*

that had the target audience 'solemnly swear to be safe around trains'.

After 44,000 Melbournites took that pledge, train safety (measured in 'near misses per million kilometres') improved by 31 per cent.

Staggeringly, those results came from a campaign with a budget of just $300,000 (AUD).

Dumb Ways to Die is typical in that it made use of (and was creatively awarded for) a vast array of executions across multiple online and offline media.

Advertising research company Warc analyse the winners of the Creative Effectiveness Lions each year, and it is clear from their work that winning campaigns exploit more channels than the other entries. They use a higher average number of channels, they make more use of social and earned media, and the number of channels they use has increased 32 per cent since 2011.

And this isn't about bigger budgets. Just like Dumb Ways to Die, many campaigns had relatively tiny budgets, but the ideas were of a nature that could powerfully spread that budget over many different channels.

Warc's research supports that of Peter Field, who found that campaigns using four or more channels performed nearly twice as well on sales growth.

Uncreative work needs to pay its way into every channel – and often in a shoe-horned way. Big creative ideas like Dumb Ways to Die naturally lend themselves to dispersement across channels – and often earn their way into channels that advertising usually can't reach.

This reality plays out in Peter's data, which shows that 92 per cent of those big, awarded ideas use four channels or more, while only 60 per cent of unawarded work does.

The most effective campaigns are also using digital more and more as lead media. While TV has declined as a media used by Creative Effectiveness winners since 2011, social, online video and mobile have all exploded, with social being the most-used lead media overall by a wide margin. And not surprisingly, the most creative campaigns much more commonly use social and online video, as uncreative work is such a difficult proposition in the online world.

So the second thing clients put on the checklist is 'will this idea work across, and earn its way into, multiple channels'.

Then what tends to happen is a discussion about what sorts of creative strategies lend themselves well to big, multichannel ideas that create fame.

Looking through the lists, it's clear that what has always been true of the best creative advertising still stands. Ideas that engage people through emotion and humour remain the bread and butter of creative effectiveness, but within that, two new themes have emerged in our digital era. Two creative strategies that seem tailor made to create fame.

1. Brands 'doing' as opposed to 'saying'

The belief that actions speak louder than words explains the marked shift in recent times from advertisers 'saying' less and 'doing' more. The tradition of advertising delivering a message is being superseded by brands proving their promise through their actions – and nowhere is this as obvious as in creative effectiveness winners.

Intermarché's 'Inglorious Fruits and Vegetables' campaign was voted France's 'favourite campaign of the year' and led to Intermarché being named France's 'favourite food retailer'. This wonderful idea saw the supermarket glorify the ugly fruit that would normally be discarded, restaging it as a worthwhile product. It led to a 24 per cent increase in sales as millions of French people dispensed with their wasteful preference for perfect looking produce. The idea was copied by other major French supermarkets, and has since spread to retailers the world over.

Rather than communicating about how fresh their fruit and vegetables were, Intermarché did something to start a completely different conversation about produce. That phenomenally effective approach can be seen in so many creative effectiveness winners.

With their Cannes Creative Effectiveness Grand Prix winning 'Guilt Trips' campaign, Australia's V/Line Trains created a new product offering. Addressing the commonality of rural Australian kids growing up, leaving home for the city, then making little effort to visit their parents, the 'Guilt Trip' was a pre-paid train ticket parents could buy for their kids. Each one came with a little piece of emotional blackmail. Ticket sales increased 15 per cent as Australians bought an extra 123,000 train rides. The idea wasn't a message. It was the solution to a well-observed customer pain point. An action from the brand that put it back on the map.

Coca-Cola's 'Share a Coke', has now won gold Effie awards in four separate global markets. The starting point was 'what can we do to the *product* to make it more desirable?' Coke is one of the all-time best at communication campaigns. But they really showed their chops with a campaign that didn't make a single promise about their product.

Inevitably, promises, claims and other marketing messages simply aren't worth talking about. "I heard the most amazing thing today. The bank I bank with said they care more about their customers than anyone else." You'd feel silly, wouldn't you? Just as actions speak louder than words, actions are much more likely to be talked about.

In a fascinating 2013 study, US innovation company Co:Collective managed to quantify the power of actions. They studied what they call 'StoryDoing©' companies – those who use actions rather than words to position their brand and tell their story. Companies such as Disney, Starbucks, American Express, JetBlue and Apple tend to turn away from traditional story-telling. They put more effort into their product and customer experience than they do persuading people with advertising and PR.

When Co:Collective compared StoryDoing© companies with the more conventional story-telling organisations, the results were stark. The StoryDoing© companies averaged almost 30-million social media mentions in 2013. The Storytelling companies? Just 5.1 million. More impressively, the StoryDoing© companies spent a quarter as much on media that same year.

The study went on to show that StoryDoing© companies had 50 per cent higher revenue growth, 200 per cent higher profit growth and 300 per cent higher share price growth.

2. Brands adopting social or environmental 'causes' as platforms

In 2013, a friend of mine commented that we seemed to be going from 'good to great to good'. He was referring to the classic Jim Collins book *Good to Great*, which found its way into the vernacular and objectives of most large companies in the 2000s. He was also referring to the much newer trend of brands doing good for the world around them.

That year, of our twelve Cases for Creativity, eight had a social cause at their heart. They weren't not for profit campaigns – rather big commercial brands using social good as a way to compel consumers.

The biggest ideas in the world that year were Dove's 'Real Beauty Sketches', Chipotle's 'Cultivate a Better World' and American Express's 'Small Business Saturday'.

Real Beauty Sketches won a gold Effie in Brazil and a Creative Effectiveness Lion for being one of the most powerful executions of Dove's long-standing Real Beauty brand platform. As the effectiveness papers contest, this reinvigoration of Dove's cause "ignited the masterbrand halo, sparking value growth in Dove's biggest categories in all four markets and significantly out-stripping category value growth in every instance."

Chipotle chose to take on the dark side of farming practices in the US with their campaign urging America to 'go back to the start' and 'cultivate a better world'. The campaign – part sustainability manifesto, part Michael Moore-esque exposé – had Americans flocking to follow its mission. Sales went up 23 per cent, while McDonalds went backwards. Since the beginning of the campaign, Chipotle's share price has climbed more than 200 per cent.[60]

Against a backdrop of huge retailers pushing small independent stores off the high streets, American Express took the side of the little guy, establishing a new national day: Small Business Saturday. A rally to get Americans 'shopping small', the initiative shot to near ubiquitous awareness. After the US Senate declared Small Business Saturday an official day, 67 per cent of the country said they would shop small, and $5.5 billion was spent with small retailers.

Of course, these benevolent campaigns aren't entirely without motive. The advertisers in question all set out with sales objectives. The ingenuity in each case was finding a cause that would advance their business. Getting consumers to choose sustainably farmed fast food would improve Chipotle's market share. Increasing the amount of money spent through American Express's payment network would increase their income.

What each advertiser understood was that consumers will latch onto, share and talk about causes they perceive as worthwhile a lot more passionately than they will about brands.

Two powerful creative strategies for generating fame: 'doing' as opposed to 'saying', and adopting social or environmental 'causes' as platforms. Both strategies that come through again and again when we look at the most creative and effective work from recent times. Both have earned their brands profitable new audiences, and their marketers much more bang for their buck. In his latest work, Peter Field reveals that 'fame' campaigns generate about one and a half times as many positive effects as other campaigns. The most interesting thing though, is that they tend to do so on less than half the budget. Clients exploiting fame get twice the efficiency of spend as those simply buying awareness.

"Whenever we have a conversation, either with the client or with ourselves in the agency, we always make sure that the audience, the consumer, is in the room with us," John Mescall told me. Now Global Executive Creative Director of McCann Worldgroup, Mescall was the Executive Creative Director at McCann Melbourne who created the Dumb Ways to Die campaign. I asked him how he got Dumb Ways to Die, such a provocative and subversive idea, approved by his client. He told me about the benchmark they use with clients: all ivory tower stuff aside, will ordinary people share this?

"Every conversation we have with our clients is about 'real world creative impact' not about theoretical marketing constructs. 'Don't look at this as a marketing person, we don't look at it as advertising practition-ers. What would a real, normal person out there, who doesn't react particularly well to most advertising, let's be honest, what would actually work with them? Will someone look at this and want to share it? Would they fall in love with it? Would they repurpose it? *Would they share it?'* And when you have those sorts of conversations where you really put the bullshit filter on, and you focus entirely on what will work in the real world, you break down a lot of barriers. You remove a key obstacle that stops a lot of people saying yes to unusual work."

In our world there is no shortage of content to share. In fact our screens are so over-populated with content that most of it won't even really be consumed. It'll be there among the tapestry of noise that sits in the background of life – a kind of screen 'muzak' that hums along innocuously, as our brains filter out everything but the most relevant or interesting.

Content isn't born with a right to be shared. Successful content *earns* a right to be shared.

What the most creative and effective work in the world demonstrates is the need to create content that is worthy of that right. To evaluate ideas based first and foremost on whether consumers will truly want to share them, rather than on those other checklists that we might hold in our heads.

After all, in a world where effectiveness is so tightly linked with fame, (in homage to Bernbach's wisdom) if your content goes unshared, everything else is academic.

TV3's *The Invisible Man*

The case for creative awards

"By the way, if anyone here is in advertising or marketing, kill yourself."
— *Bill Hicks*

There are few things more galling to creative sceptics than ineffective campaigns winning creative awards. Why would we award campaigns on any basis other than their effectiveness? Advertising's got one job, and that's to sell stuff. If it doesn't, then what does it matter how 'creative' it is?

Effectiveness awards have a clear value. They celebrate the prosperity of our clients and reward the agency's role in that success. Increasingly, creative awards are following suit – most award-entry case study videos now come complete with effectiveness measures at the end.

I think this represents a healthy maturing of our industry – but I also fear for us losing the celebration of simply exploring new creative frontiers. I say this because, while effectiveness awards are fantastic for acknowledging what's worked, creative awards play a very different role, and a critically important one, in advancing the effectiveness of our industry.

In 2001, my old agency Colenso BBDO won a silver Cannes Lion for a stunt promoting a TV show called *The Invisible Man*. They'd sent a trained dog into a public place to walk around on its own with a stiffened leash protruding from its neck as if it were being walked by an invisible man. The stunt brought a smile to the faces of the hundred or so people who saw it, and made for a great photo to be entered into creative awards.

I remember people being a little outraged that this 'scammy' stunt had won an award. They rightfully pointed out that the stunt, being executed on such a tiny scale, could not possibly have meaningfully affected viewership of the show.

But this was actually an important idea for the agency and the industry. It happened at a time when we were just beginning to learn about communicating outside of traditional media. The internet had arrived and TV and magazines were beginning to decline, and for the good of our clients we had to change with those times and learn how to broaden our canvas.

The Invisible Man stunt was part of a crucial process of learning how to create experiential advertising and drive word of mouth. Back then, those skills couldn't simply be acquired – they need to be learned and honed.

Six years later when I joined the agency they were dining out on the awards success of another stunt. This one was for a courier company called Deadline. The idea sought to demonstrate how seriously Deadline took their promise of when a package would be delivered. "When we give you a time, we mean it", they assured. So the agency strapped explosives to a billboard. The headline "This message will self destruct in exactly:" appeared over a huge countdown timer in the centre of the billboard. And at the end of a month of counting down, sure enough, the billboard exploded. This time, the visibility was much higher, with thousands of commuters seeing the campaign and the media reporting around the explosion. Again a part of the process of learning new skills – 'doing' rather than saying, and courting the media to help drive fame.

Those new skills culminated in 2009 with a campaign that became the most awarded campaign, for both creativity and effectiveness, that New Zealand had ever produced.

A year earlier we'd been briefed by Yellow Pages to help them transform their brand. They were known as the big yellow book that your parents got out of the cupboard under the telephone when something went wrong with the toilet. And they were being eaten by Google. Yellow needed people to believe that they were better than Google if you were searching for businesses. And we'd found some evidence that this was true. At the time, only half of New Zealand's small businesses had a web presence of their own that would show up in a Google search. But almost every single one could

Deadline Couriers' *Exploding Billboard*

148

Yellow's *Treehouse Restaurant*

be found on Yellow's website, mobile app and book. So if you needed to get something done, you were much more likely to find the help you needed by searching Yellow than by searching Google.

To demonstrate the comprehensiveness of Yellow's business listings, we challenged an ordinary woman from Auckland to build a treehouse restaurant using only the Yellow Pages website and mobile app. As she completed this amazing feat, starting by finding a tree and finishing by hosting a spectacular dining experience for 2,000 people from across the world, New Zealanders got to see just how useful the Yellow Pages could be, even for the most imaginative jobs, and even in 2009.

During the campaign, Yellow New Zealand became the only Yellow Pages business in the world to take share of search back from Google. The campaign won every creative award under the sun. It also won nine different effectiveness awards, both in New Zealand and abroad, including Platinum at the Asian Marketing Effectiveness Awards for the most effective campaign anywhere in Asia Pacific in 2009. On his retirement in 2010, after 40 years in the agency, Colenso's founder Roger MacDonnell named Treehouse the campaign he was most proud of from the agency's entire history.

It was a highly sophisticated and largely experiential integrated campaign – one we never could have pulled off had we not been experimenting in the years earlier with things like the Invisible Man and the Exploding Billboard. Nor could our entire industry have evolved toward campaigns like Share A Coke, Dumb Ways to Die or Small Business Saturday without learning from each other all manner of new techniques showcased at creative awards over preceding years.

While it was accurate at the time to point out that the dog on the leash can't have been particularly effective, it was wholly short sighted to claim that it was of no value.

And this is the point about creative awards. Effectiveness awards tell us what was effective in the past. Creative awards help us collectively understand what will be effective in the future. They help us continually hone our craft and inspire us forward. In a world that's so constantly changing, our industry needs to be in a continual state of learning. If we weren't, our work would become less and less effective.

Fussing about whether creative awards are good or bad is a poor use of our energies. It is much smarter to use the outcomes of creative awards to learn and inspire. To glimpse the future of advertising, and to apply those new techniques. To move forward more quickly, more effectively, and more creatively.

After all, creativity is good for business. It makes companies more successful by making their advertising far more effective in delivering a return on their investment.

The 15 industry and academic studies covered in this book represent two decades of research comparing the effects of a more creative approach with a less creative one. They represent not only a correlation between more creative advertising and more effective advertising, but also a deep understanding of exactly how creativity makes advertising more effective – from making it stand out more, to making it more likely to be recalled, to getting it talked about more and finally to making it more persuasive.

What makes the case all the more compelling is the absence of contrary research. If there is a case against creativity, it's extremely difficult to find. Every one of the dozens of university academics and industry professionals who have explored this topic has arrived at the same conclusion – that a more creative approach is a much surer path to success.

The wonderful thing about creativity is that it isn't only good for business. It's also good for people.

The same is difficult to say for advertising in general. "Advertising is a racket," said F. Scott Fitzgerald. "you cannot be honest without admitting that its constructive contribution to humanity is exactly minus zero."

Even advertising legend David Ogilvy sympathised. "As a private person," he said, "I have a passion for landscape, and I have never seen one improved by a billboard. When I retire from Madison Avenue, I am going to start a secret society of masked vigilantes who will travel around the world on silent motorbicycles, chopping down posters at the dark of the moon. How many juries will convict us when we are caught in these acts of beneficent citizenship?"

And it's something of an irony that Bill Hicks, the American comedian who's among the most adored by advertising creatives, is perhaps their most vehement detractor.

"By the way, if anyone here is in advertising or marketing," he famously ranted on stage in the early

1990s, "Kill yourself. Seriously though, if you are, do. You think there's going to be a joke coming. There's no joke coming. You are Satan's spawn, filling the world with bile and garbage. Kill yourself."

Hicks' tongue was sharper than most, but his views aren't necessarily extreme. A recent study showed that 65 per cent of consumers feel "constantly bombarded" with advertising and that 60 per cent have a "much more negative opinion toward advertising than they did a few years ago".[61]

Far be it from me to suggest that we have any sort of responsibility to not fill the world with bile and garbage (as Howard Gossage once said "to explain responsibility to advertising men is like trying to convince an eight-year-old that sexual intercourse is more fun than a chocolate ice cream cone"). But, maybe, electing to keep the advertising landscape beautiful mightn't be quite the hippie ideology that it sounds. Gallup & Robinson recently found that consumers who felt better about advertising in general tended to recall and be persuaded by specific advertisements more than those with negative attitudes toward advertising.[62] What they showed was that if we improve the overall palatability of advertising, we will improve the ROI we see on our advertising spend. So it's very much in our commercial interests not to fill the world with bile and garbage.

And furthermore, isn't it brilliant when we can achieve success for our clients while at the same time contributing something of value to the world around us?

And I don't mean Corporate Social Responsibility marketing. I mean creativity.

When we produced the Yellow Treehouse campaign, we anticipated a campaign that would garner media attention and make a difference to our client's business. It did that in droves, but what we had not anticipated was just how much consumers who engaged with the campaign would get out of it. While the restaurant was open, we were inundated with notes from people who had eaten dinner inside our ad campaign and had the time of their lives doing it.

"We ate at the Treehouse on the 17th," wrote one diner, "and the whole evening was magical from start to finish. It was a unique experience that will never be forgotten. Thank you."

"What a fabulous experience," said another. "The food was fantastic, the service brilliant – and the location, well, a once in a lifetime experience."

A third had her birthday in the tree. "We feel it was a privilege to be able to come and visit the place. Thank you for making our day so perfect and the start of my fiftieth year something extra special."

The Yellow Treehouse wasn't a social marketing campaign, a charity campaign or a campaign for another 'good cause'. It was a regular old 'selling' campaign for a commercial organisation wanting more people to use its products. And yet it managed to make that happen without filling the world with more bile and garbage.

Making advertising's great. Making advertising that works, even better. But making advertising that works by contributing something of value to people is by far the best thing we can do. Why? Because as it turns out, consumers think much more of those companies that chose to advertise without the bile and garbage.

Agnosticism notwithstanding, my favourite quote of all time comes from the thirteenth-century French Roman Catholic friar, Saint Francis of Assisi.

"Preach the Gospel at all times," he counselled his brothers. "Use words if necessary."

His insight was that people infer things about you not only from what you say, but even more so from what you do and how you do it. That there is unspoken communication, and that others often pay more attention to this than they do to the words we speak.

It took 750 years for behavioural psychology to catch up with Saint Francis, but in 1967, three American psychologists found that what they termed meta communication (i.e. the non-verbal emotive paraphernalia that accompanies what was being said) was far more potent at influencing interpersonal relationships than the content of the communication. In simple terms, changing what people said had little influence on how they felt about one another, but changing how they said it had a big influence.[63]

It is as true for advertising as it is for any form of communication. Research has shown that consumers' responses to advertising are formed not only by the message in the advertising, but also by the variables of how that message is delivered. For example, how much money is spent on delivering it.

"Advertising expense is an indicator of marketing effort," wrote a small tweed of academics from the Stockholm School of Economics in 2008. "The more

St Francis of Assisi

money spent on advertising, the greater the effort, meaning that the advertiser must really believe in the product. Spending a great deal of money on advertising is a more powerful signal to consumers about the quality of the product than the content of the advertising, as the advertiser has 'put their money where their mouth is'. More money means greater risk, and thus consumers feel safe that the advertiser will deliver on their promise."

Intrigued by the effects of the unspoken, those academics went on to publish a further study on another form of unspoken communication – creativity.

"We expect that greater creativity signals more effort (as creative advertising is harder to produce) and thus produces more favourable brand perceptions."

They hypothesised that beyond helping a message stand out and persuade, creativity had yet another positive effect; that companies that went to the trouble of being creative would be thought better of by consumers.

They studied over 1,200 people aged 18 to 65, showing them both creative and uncreative advertising, and then measuring the differences in how that advertising made them feel about the companies being advertised.

The findings were extraordinary. They discovered that more creative advertising, regardless of whether the creativity was at all relevant to the selling message, had a far greater impact than less creative advertising on consumers' positive perceptions of the company being advertised.

Compared with less creative advertising for the same company, the more creative advertising made people conclude that the company had gone to a greater effort for them (52 per cent higher for creative advertising), that the company was smarter (69 per cent higher), that the company developed more valuable products (50 per cent higher), that the company was better at solving problems (83 per cent higher), that the company's products were of a higher quality (36 per cent higher), that the company was worthy of their interest (88 per cent higher), and that the company's products were worth purchasing (73 per cent higher).[64]

When we choose to be more creative with our advertising, we don't just improve our chances of communicating its message. We send a second and perhaps even louder message to consumers that we are a smarter company with better products. A company that takes pride in the things it does and strives for excellence. When we choose to be less creative, we communicate the opposite. One wonders how many well-intentioned messages have gone to waste having been out-shouted by uncreative delivery.

And yet, uncreative delivery still appears to make a case for itself. So many traditional, sensible campaigns win at the effectiveness awards. And if creativity's so effective, why aren't all those shiny campaigns we see at creative awards getting Effies?

While effectiveness award shows tend to be dominated by big campaigns for big brands with big media budgets, creative award shows tend to be the opposite. They are usually dominated by smaller campaigns, often for smaller brands, and usually with smaller media allocations.

The reason for this, of course, is that when there is less to lose, clients are willing to be more creative. It's the campaign for the pro-bono client that had production and media resources donated. It's the campaign for the large corporation's smallest product line. It's the single maverick execution among a much bigger and less creative campaign. It's the fringes.

At creative award shows we celebrate the bleeding edge of experimentalism, of entrepreneurialism, of innovation in advertising. And the fringes are usually where agencies do their most innovative work, because those fringes are where clients feel most comfortable taking the greatest risks.

An unfortunate side effect is that effectiveness is rarely measured at the fringes. Large campaigns for large brands get measured. The client has funding and systems in place for measurement, and a need to prove the return on such a large investment. Measurement, being an expensive exercise, is rarely affordable for small campaigns or small brands, and as a campaign gets smaller, isolating its effects from everything else going on in the market becomes exponentially more difficult and expensive.

With adequate resourcing we might find that those small, award-winning campaigns are in fact highly effective. After all, lack of an Effie is not evidence that a campaign has been ineffective. But alas, in most cases we are doomed never to know.

The ingrained logic tells us that we are best not to risk it. Why ask the agency for a highly creative campaign and risk it not working when you could ask them for a less creative one and have a surer shot at success?

However, two decades of research shows this to be a misconception, and one that makes ineffective advertising all too common. Each year, we choose to be uncreative most of the time, and we choose to spend more money on those uncreative campaigns than we do on the creative ones. Those campaigns go on to be, on average, much less effective than the creatively awarded ones. And because we have spent more money on them, return on marketing investment is seriously diminished.

Yes it is true that, among the hundreds of thousands of campaigns produced worldwide each year, examples exist of creatively awarded campaigns being ineffective. But while we earnestly try to lessen those instances, it is important to remember just how tremendously uncommon they are.

The research shows that for every 50,000 campaigns, just one will win a creative award without producing a business result. By contrast, just shy of 15,000 uncreative campaigns will deliver no return to their advertiser. And the remaining 34,995 uncreative campaigns that do achieve a measurable result will be less effective than their creatively awarded counterparts.

FOR EVERY 50,000 ADVERTISING CAMPAIGNS PRODUCED

7	**49,993**
will achieve a creative award	will not achieve a creative award
6	**34,995**
will achieve both a creative award and, on average, a larger business result	will not achieve a creative award, and will achieve, on average, a smaller business result
1	**14,998**
will achieve a creative award but not a business result	will achieve neither a creative award nor a business result

(1 in 7,000 campaigns produced achieve a creative award,[65] advertising in general has been shown to achieve a business result 70% of the time,[66] and creatively-awarded advertising has been shown to achieve a business result 84% of the time.[67])

Highly creative but ineffective work is extremely rare, but very noticeable because it wins awards.

What's less noticeable, but without doubt of far greater cost to the business community, is the gargantuan amount of uncreative advertising that creates no return on its investment. We're bombarded with it every day of our lives. This is the advertising we have grown so capable of tuning out of that we don't even notice it anymore. The 2,998 ads that you can't recall from the last 24 hours. Clients of our industry spend billions and billions of dollars on them each year.

Call me crazy, but shouldn't that be the problem we're working to solve?

The 15 Studies

The question of whether a more creative approach is a more effective one has been asked by dozens of people from industry insiders and university academics to the likes of McKinsey & Company. The studies span three decades and are from all corners of the world. They ask the same question, but in 15 different ways. And every one reaches the same conclusion.

These are the studies that constitute *The Case for Creativity*:

1   Creative Advertising and the Von Restorff Effect

Psychological Reports, 1991

Psychologists Pick, Sweeney and Clay demonstrate that creativity enhances consumers' unaided recall of advertising.

2   On Resonance: A Critical Pluralistic Inquiry into Advertising Rhetoric

Journal of Consumer Research, 1992

McQuarrie and Mick show that creativity in the form of word-play, ambiguity and incongruity increases liking for an ad, improves brand attitude, and increases unaided recall.

3   Creativity vs Effectiveness? An Integrating Classification for Advertising

Journal of Advertising Research, 1995

Kover, Goldberg and James, Fordham University, New York, show that creativity facilitates and increases purchase intention, and that campaigns that work at an emotional level are more effective than those that appeal rationally.

4 Do Award-Winning Commercials Sell?

Leo Burnett, 1996

Donald Gunn shows creatively awarded campaigns to be effective in 86.5 per cent of cases. This study was repeated in 2002, with a result of 82 per cent effectiveness.

5 Recall, Liking and Creativity in TV Commercials: A New Approach

Journal of Advertising Research, 2000

Stone, Besser and Lewis of Southern Illinois University, show well-liked advertising to be much more likely to be creative, and conclude that "there is a much better chance of breaking through the clutter with a creative offering".

6 Breaking Through the Clutter: Benefits of Advertisement Originality and Familiarity for Brand Attention and Memory

Management Science, 2002

In which Pieters, Warlop and Wedel of Tilburg University, the Netherlands, show that more original advertising commands greater attention and achieves greater recall.

7 Recall and Persuasion: Does Creative Advertising Matter?

Journal of Advertising, 2005

Till and Baack, of the University of South Carolina, show that creatively awarded advertising is much more likely to be recalled than advertising in general.

8 Marketing in the Era of Accountability

Institute of Practitioners in Advertising, 2007

Binet and Field show that campaigns that appeal to the emotions and drive word of mouth are the most effective.

9 Art Meets Science: Creative Advertising Examined

Power Brands: Measuring, Making, and Managing Brand Success, 2007

In which McKinsey & Company consultants Hajo Riesenbeck and Jesko Perrey show that more creative campaigns are effective more often than less-creative campaigns.

10 The Impact of Advertising Creativity on the Hierarchy of Effects

Journal of Advertising, 2008

In which Smith, Chen and Yang of the Universities of Indiana and Wisconsin-Milwaukee show that creative ads attract more attention, create more brand awareness, aid with depth of processing, are more memorable, and most interestingly, reduce consumers' resistance to persuasion.

11 Advertising Creativity Matters

Journal of Advertising Research, 2008

In which Dahlén, Rosengren and Törn of the Stockholm School of Economics show that creative advertising makes consumers think better of the companies that produce that advertising.

12 Creative = Effective

Campaign Brief, 2008 (First published in Campaign Brief, 2008, and repeated in 2011 and 2015 for Chapter Two of this book.) James Hurman shows that creatively focused agencies more efficiently produce more effective advertising.

13 Beyond Attention Effects: Modelling the Persuasive and Emotional Effects of Advertising Creativity

Marketing Science, 2009

Yang and Smith of the Universities of Wisconsin-Milwaukee and Indiana show that highly creative advertising triggers greater open-mindedness, making consumers more willing to buy, as opposed to be cynical about, the marketing message contained within the advertising.

14 Creative = Successful

NZ Marketing, 2010 (First published in *NZ Marketing*, 2010, and updated in 2011 and 2015 for Chapter Seven of this book.) In which James Hurman shows that the Cannes Advertiser of the Year and Creative Marketer of the Year companies all experienced extraordinary share market performances during the period of their Cannes Lion-winning campaigns.

15 The Link Between Creativity and Effectiveness

Institute of Practitioners in Advertising, 2010 (First published by the IPA, 2010, and updated in 2011 and 2016.) Peter Field shows that creative award-winning campaigns are significantly more effective than non-creative award-winning campaigns.

The aim of this book is to share with you the discoveries made in those studies. And for you in turn to be able to share them with others. To help that along, there is a short presentation of the main points available at THECASEFORCREATIVITY.COM – with any luck it is a practical way to illustrate the value of creativity to those around us, be they advertising people, marketers, or folks from any other walk of business life.

Download it, cut it up, add bits in, pass it off as your own work, whatever does it for you. Find a way to use it to make better, more creative, more effective advertising.

JAMES HURMAN

Image credits

CHAPTER ONE

'BMX' photo courtesy of Ben Couzens

'Times Square' photo by Terabass, used under Creative Commons license (http://creativecommons.org/licenses/by-sa/3.0/deed.en)

CHAPTER THREE

'Banana' image courtesy of Wieden+ Kennedy/Honda, photography by Paul Zac

CHAPTER FOUR

'Godmarks' photo by Chuck "Caveman" Coker, used under Creative Commons license (http://creativecommons.org/licenses/by-nd/2.0/)

'Vodafone Symphonia' photo courtesy of Colenso BBDO/Vodafone; 'AKQA Christmas Video' photo courtesy of AKQA

'David' photo by Rico Heil, used under Creative Commons license (http://creativecommons.org/licenses/by-sa/3.0/deed.en); 'Hermes' photo by roccuz, used under Creative Commons license (http://creativecommons.org/licenses/by-sa/2.5/it/deed.en)

CHAPTER SIX

'Bill Bernbach' photo courtesy of DDB

CHAPTER EIGHT

'Coca Cola Bottles' photo by Katja Ullrich, used under Creative Commons license (https://creativecommons.org/licenses/by-sa/3.0/deed.en)

'Small Business Saturday' photo by Elvert Barnes, used under Creative Commons license (https://creativecommons.org/licenses/by-sa/2.0/)

CHAPTER NINE

'Invisible Man', 'Exploding Billboard' and 'Yellow Treehouse' photos courtesy of Colenso BBDO

Saint Francis of Assisi, Francisco de Zurbarán, c.1658

Acknowledgements

My heartfelt thanks to everybody who helped make this book happen:

Scott Bedbury, Ashley Bellview, Simon Bird, Michael Conrad, Ben Couzens, Nick Cullen, Tony Davidson, Peter Field, Nick Garrett, Donald Gunn, Soren Hagh, Olivia Johnson, David Lubars, Michael Lynch, Jim McDowell, James McGrath, Jonathan Mildenhall, Jim Moser, Ben Neumayr, Huw O'Connor, Paul Rees-Jones, Fred Senn, Jim Stengel, Bruce Tait, Joe Thomson, Suresh Vittal, Scott Wallace, Matt Whetherly and Emma Wilkie.

To the publisher of the original 2011 edition, AUT Media, especially Vincent Heeringa, who took a leap of faith getting this pet project of mine off the ground and was so graciously supportive of this new edition.

To the publisher of this edition, Cannes Lions, especially David Davies who has, with absolute British grace and composure, seen this new book out at record speed. Also to Philip Thomas and Terry Savage who have welcomed and supported me in so many ways over the years.

To Kelvin Soh and SonLa Pham of DD/MM/YY, the design firm I turn to whenever I need something done beyond perfectly, and who designed the book you are now holding.

To Keith Weed for generously giving his time to write the foreword.

To the great planner and wonderful champion of creative effectiveness Tim Broadbent, who helped me a great deal with the first edition, and sadly passed away as I was working on this updated edition.

To those people who were my most inspiring creative teachers and partners during my years in advertising – Josh Moore, Paul McElwain, David Thomason, Brent Smart and Nick Worthington.

And finally to my beloved wife Annabel and our children Tripp and Harper. If ever there were a case for creativity…

Endnotes

CHAPTER ONE

1   Couzens & Ingram's 'Wicked Sick Project' (carried out at George Patterson y&r Melbourne) is tidily and entertainingly summarised in a case study video that can be found at http://www.youtube.com/watch?v=Cd6-n7MhVg8

2   J. Walker Smith, former president of the consulting firm Yankelovich, told *USA Today* in 2006 that the average 1970s city dweller was exposed to 500–2,000 ad messages a day, and that now it's 3,000 to 5,000. For several more thought-provoking statistics on the saturation of marketing messages, read 'Product placement: you can't escape it' at http://www.usatoday.com/money/advertising/2006-10-10-ad-nauseum-usat_x.htm

3   Raymond A. Bauer and Stephen A. Greyser of Harvard University's Graduate School of Business Administration asked people to count the advertisements to which they paid at least some attention, finding that each day brings 76 advertisements of which a person is to some degree aware – *Advertising in America: The Consumer View* (1964). Charles F. Adams, working with the Bauer and Greyser data in 1965, emphasised that of the 76 advertisements a day of which a person might be aware, only 12 made any kind of impression – *Common Sense in Advertising* (1965). And my own research showed that people could recall an average of 1.7 ads from the last 24 hours.

4   Academic researchers commonly discuss the schism between creatively-focused and effectiveness-focused agency people in their papers. One such paper is 'Creativity vs Effectiveness? An Integrating Classification for Advertising' by Kover, Goldberg & James, which can be sourced from https://www.researchgate.net/publication/259346472_Creativity_versus_Effectiveness_An_Integrating_Classification_for_Advertising

5   This unattributed and rather premature verdict was stated in the book *Power Brands: Measuring, Making, and Managing Brand Success* (2007, p.25) by McKinsey consultants Hajo Riesenbeck and Jesko Perrey.

6   A quick calculation of the number of campaigns booked by the UK's media companies and the number of UK campaigns that win a creative award each year reveals approximately 1 in 7,000 to be creatively awarded. It's worth noting that the UK is one of the most creative advertising markets in the world, and so the figure would likely be even more weighted toward uncreative campaigns if calculated globally. 'The Link Between Creativity and Effectiveness', p7 – http://blog.grey.de/wp-content/uploads/2011/10/Creativity_and_Effectiveness_Report.pdf

7   You can watch an excellent series of presentations, including Tess Alps' introduction and Peter Field's 'The Link Between Creativity and Effectiveness' at http://uat.thinkbox.tv/server/show/nav.1320

CHAPTER TWO

Chapter Two is an expansion on an article entitled 'Creative = Effective', which first appeared in *Campaign Brief* magazine, January 2008

8 'Are Advertising Creative Awards really Worth the Cost?' by Lisa Sanders, *Advertising Age*, 15 June 2006. http://adage.com/article/cannes06/advertising-creative-awards-worth-cost/109918/

9 'Pitch Secrets: How Clients Really Think' by Martin Jones, *Campaign*, 20 March 2009. http://www.campaignlive.co.uk/news/892385/Pitch-Secrets-clients-really-think/?DCMP=ILC-SEARCH

10 'Commercial Art Must Be Both' by Eric Hirshberg, *Creativity*, 25 August 2008. http://creativity-online.com/news/commercial-art-must-be-both/130130

CHAPTER THREE

11 If you haven't read UK advertising luminary Jeremy Bullmore's column 'On the Campaign Couch' then you should. This particular quote came from the 18 September 2009 edition: http://www.campaignlive.co.uk/news/941068/Opinion-campaign-couch-JB/?DCMP=ILC-SEARCH

12 As of February 2011, BBDO was Network of the year at Cannes for the fourth year running, #1 Network in the Big Won report for the fourth year running and Most Awarded Agency Network in the World in the Gunn report for the fifth year running.

13 'Creative Enough for the Finance Director' by Millward Brown's Andy Farr and Sue Gardiner, *Admap*, March 2001

14 Richard Huntington's blog, and particularly the post that this quote came from, are great. http://www.adliterate.com/archives/2008/03/the_four_is_2.html

15 'Ideas are just a multiplier of execution' by Derek Sivers. http://sivers.org/multiply

16 John Hegarty in AdWeek - http://www.adweek.com/news/advertising-branding/love-hate-and-great-work-john-hegarty-and-dan-wieden-141310

CHAPTER FOUR

Chapter Four is an adaptation of the articles 'We are not here to do what has already been done', which first appeared in *Idealog* magazine, January/February 2007 and 'Casualties of Coincidence', which first appeared in *Idealog* magazine, July/August 2010.

18 Colenso BBDO's Vodafone 'Symphonia' TV commercial can be seen at http://www. youtube.com/watch?v=r3nSoEhy8SM

19 The 'Happy Christmas from AKQA' video, eerily similar to our Vodafone spot, can be seen at http://www.youtube.com/watch?v=FgBUqJzgwBo

20 I would like to thank Maggie Antone for introducing me to Malcolm Gladwell's article 'In the Air: Who Says Big Ideas Are Rare'. The article didn't make it into *What the Dog Saw*, Malcolm's collection of *New Yorker* articles, but it's a must-read for the Gladwell obscurist, and freely available at http://www.newyorker.com/reporting/2008/05/12/080512fa_fact_gladwell

21   When Smith, Chen & Yang catalogued the academic research into creativity for their 2008 *Journal of Advertising* paper 'The Impact of Advertising Creativity on the Hierarchy of Effects' they found five studies that concluded that "creative ads enhance consumers' unaided recall of ad ideas", thereby showing that original advertising stands out more, both in the media landscape and later in the mind: Pick, Sweeney & Clay, 1991; McQuarrie & Mick, 1992; Stewart & Furse, 2000; Pieters, Warlop & Wedel, 2002; Till & Baack, 2005.

22   Box Office Mojo's 'All Time Box Office' list evolves constantly, but each time I revisit it I find the same glut of unoriginal cinema and a dearth of truly new stories. See if that still holds true today at http://www.boxofficemojo.com/alltime/world/

23   Like reading about the childhood of a celebrity, it's pleasantly voyeuristic to peruse the genesis of Dove's 'Campaign for Real Beauty', one of the most famous advertising efforts of the 2000s. 'The Real Truth About Beauty' is available at http://www.clubofamsterdam.com/contentarticles/52%20Beauty/dove_white_paper_final.pdf

24   For a long time I had a hunch that advertising arguments lost momentum over time as people thought their way out of them, so I was delighted to find the work of social psychologists John T. Cacioppo and Richard E. Petty. They explored and proved the fascinating notion that people have a tendency to develop counter-arguments over time.

That work was described in 'Effects of Message Repetition and Position on Cognitive Response, Recall and Persuasion' from the *Journal of Personality and Social Psychology*, volume 37, 1979.

25   'The Impact of Advertising Creativity on the Hierarchy of Effects' by Smith, Chen & Yang, *Journal of Advertising*, Winter 2008.

CHAPTER FIVE

26   Thank you to Donald Gunn who generously took the time to post me his seminal, and pre-internet study, 'Do Award-winning Commercials Sell?'

27   I hope that I have done 'The Link Between Creativity and Effectiveness' justice in my retelling of its story. The original and very brilliant debrief remains available at http://blog.grey.de/wp-content/uploads/2011/10/Creativity_and_Effectiveness_Report.pdf

28   The McKinsey & Company study, 'Art Meets Science: Creative Advertising Examined', *Power Brands: Measuring, Making, and Managing Brand Success* (2007, p25).

29   Vault.com, a leading career intelligence firm, periodically ranks management consulting firms according to their prestige and standing within the business community. McKinsey & Company was #1 on that list in 2011 and had held that position for six consecutive years.

CHAPTER SIX

30   'Breaking Through the Clutter: Benefits of Advertisement Originality and Familiarity for Brand Attention and Memory' by Pieters, Warlop

& Wedel, Tilburg University, Netherlands, published in *Management Science,* June 2002

31 Pick, Sweeney & Clay, 1991; McQuarrie & Mick, 1992; Stewart & Furse, 2000; Pieters, Warlop & Wedel, 2002; Till & Baack, 2005.

32 'Recall & Persuasion: Does Creative Advertising Matter?' by Till & Baack, University of South Carolina, USA, published in *Journal of Advertising*, Fall 2005.

33 'Beyond Attention Effects: Modeling the Persuasive and Emotional Effects of Advertising Creativity' by Yang & Smith, Universities of Wisconsin-Milwaukee and Indiana, published in *Marketing Science*, September/October 2009

CHAPTER SEVEN

Chapter Seven is an adaptation of the study 'Creative = Successful', which first appeared in NZ Marketing magazine, March/April 2010.

34 Volkswagen's share data is available at http://finance.yahoo.com/q?s=VOW.DE

35 The S&P 500 growth figures quoted are the average across the two years preceding Volkswagen being crowned Advertiser of the year. The average S&P 500 growth across 2007 (5.49 per cent) and 2008 (-37 per cent) was -15.8 per cent.

36 Sony share data is available at http://finance.yahoo.com/q?s=SNE&ql=0

37 Anheuser-Busch share data is available at http://finance.yahoo.com/q?s=BUD

38 Swatch share data is available at http://www.swatchgroup.com/investor_relations/share_quotes

39 Nike Annual report 2002 Chairman's Letter to Shareholders – http://media.corporate-ir.net/media_files/irol/10/100529/Areports/ar_02/letter.html

40 BMW Films Sales Information – http://en.wikipedia.org/wiki/BMW_Films

41 BMW share data is available at http://finance.yahoo.com/q?s=BMW.DE&ql=0

42 PlayStation Sales Information – http://en.wikipedia.org/wiki/PlayStation_2

43 Adidas share data is available at http://finance.yahoo.com/q?s=ADS.DE&ql=0

44 Adidas 'Impossible is Nothing Campaign Case Study' – http://http://marketing-case-studies.blogspot.co.uk/2008/01/impossible-is-nothing-campaign.html

45 Honda share data is available at http://finance.yahoo.com/q?s=HMC

46 Honda's IPA Effectiveness Gold winning paper 'What Happened When Honda Started Asking Questions?' isn't in the public domain, but if you've got a Warc account, just search the title.

47 P&G share data is available at http://finance.yahoo.com/q?s=pg

48 'P&G Share Price Soars' – http://www.highbeam.com/doc/1G1-171927331.html

49 Unilever share data is available at https://nz.finance.yahoo.com/echarts?s=ULVR.L#symbol=ULVR.L;range=my

50 Mars are notoriously tight about sharing figures and results, although Forbes provides a smattering here – http://www.forbes.com/lists/2011/21/private-companies-11_Mars_L600.html

51 Ikea's 2010 Yearly Summary can be found at http://www.ikea.com/ms/en_US/pdf/yearly_summary/ys_welcome_inside_2010.pdf

52 Coca-Cola share data is available at https://nz.finance.yahoo.com/echarts?s=KO#symbol=KO;range=my

53 McDonald's share data is available at https://nz.finance.yahoo.com/echarts?s=MCD

54 Heineken share data is available at https://nz.finance.yahoo.com/echarts?s=HEIA.AS#symbol=HEIA.AS;range=my

55 Here, Mr Stengel is referring to Donald Gunn's 'Do Award-winning Commercials Sell?' study – carried out at Leo Burnett during the period when Michael Conrad was Chief Creative Officer of Leo Burnett Worldwide.

56 Watch Coca-Cola's 'Content 2020' film here: https://www.youtube.com/watch?v=LerdMmWjU_E

57 *How Disruption Brought Order* by Jean-Marie Dru (2007), p.214.

58 See Adidas's impressive growth through the 2000s in their 2009 Annual report – http://www.adidas-group.com/media/filer_public/2013/07/31/gb_2009_en.pdf

CHAPTER EIGHT

All campaign effectiveness data is from Effie or Cannes Creative Effectiveness Lions entry papers, which have been independently validated. These papers are available to Warc subscribers at warc.com

59 You can find all the Bullets from Gunn at http://www.gunnreport.com/content/bullets-from-gunn/ and all the Cases for Creativity at http://www.gunnreport.com/content/cases-for-creativity/

60 Chipotle share data is available at https://nz.finance.yahoo.com/echarts?s=CMG#symbol=CMG;range=my

CHAPTER NINE

61 'Drowned in Advertising Chatter: The Case for Regulating Ad Time on Television' – https://litigation-essentials.lexisnexis.com/webcd/app?action=DocumentDisplay&crawlid=1&srctype=smi&srcid=3B15&doctype=cite&docid=94+Geo.+L.J.+1229&key=401302a1a7437bab0ecbd5ab8c75b216

62 Gallup & Robinson's May 2000 *Journal of Advertising Research* paper 'Advertising Attitudes and Advertising Effectiveness' concluded that "advertising performance is influenced by consumers' attitudes toward advertising in general. Respondents with more favourable attitudes toward advertising recalled a higher number of advertisements the day after exposure and were more persuaded by them."

63 I borrowed Heath, Nairn & Bottomley's eloquent description of metacommunication, from their paper 'How Effective is Creativity? Emotive Content in TV Advertising Does Not Increase Attention', published in the *Journal of Advertising Research*, December 2009. The original 1967 research is available in 'Pragmatics of Human Communication' by Watzlawick, Bavelas, & Jackson.

64 'Advertising Creativity Matters', Dahlén, Rosengren & Törn, published in *Journal of Advertising Research*, Vol. 48, No. 3, Sept 2008.

65 'The Link Between Creativity and Effectivness', p7 – http://blog.grey.de/wp-content/uploads/2011/10/Creativity_and_Effectiveness_Report.pdf

66 The work of John Phillip Jones in the USA, Colin McDonald in the UK and Burckhard Brandes in Germany, summarised in 'Pre-testing Methods: The Agony of Choice' by Tim Broadbent, Admap Magazine, October 1997.

67 'Do Award-winning Commercials Sell?' – www.gunnreport.com